American Tales

A MUSICAL IN TWO ACTS,
BASED ON STORIES BY CLASSIC
AMERICAN WRITERS

Book and Lyrics by
Ken Stone

Music by
Jan Powell

A SAMUEL FRENCH ACTING EDITION

FOUNDED 1830

New York Hollywood London Toronto

SAMUELFRENCH.COM

Book & Lyrics copyright © 2008, 2009 by Ken Stone
Cover Artwork Design by Charity Capili

ALL RIGHTS RESERVED

CAUTION: Professionals and amateurs are hereby warned that *AMERICAN TALES* is subject to a royalty. It is fully protected under the copyright laws of the United States of America, the British Commonwealth, including Canada, and all other countries of the Copyright Union. All rights, including professional, amateur, motion picture, recitation, lecturing, public reading, radio broadcasting, television and the rights of translation into foreign languages are strictly reserved. In its present form the play is dedicated to the reading public only.

The amateur live stage performance rights to *AMERICAN TALES* are controlled exclusively by Samuel French, Inc., and royalty arrangements and licenses must be secured well in advance of presentation. PLEASE NOTE that amateur royalty fees are set upon application in accordance with your producing circumstances. When applying for a royalty quotation and license please give us the number of performances intended, dates of production, your seating capacity and admission fee. Royalties are payable one week before the opening performance of the play to Samuel French, Inc., at 45 W. 25th Street, New York, NY 10010.

Royalty of the required amount must be paid whether the play is presented for charity or gain and whether or not admission is charged.

Stock royalty quoted upon application to Samuel French, Inc.

For all other rights than those stipulated above, apply to: Gage Group, 14724 Ventura Blvd., #505, Sherman Oaks, CA 91403 Attn: Martin Gage.

Particular emphasis is laid on the question of amateur or professional readings, permission and terms for which must be secured in writing from Samuel French, Inc.

Copying from this book in whole or in part is strictly forbidden by law, and the right of performance is not transferable.

Whenever the play is produced the following notice must appear on all programs, printing and advertising for the play: "Produced by special arrangement with Samuel French, Inc."

Due authorship credit must be given on all programs, printing and advertising for the play.

ISBN 978-0-573-69619-0   Printed in U.S.A.   #29031

No one shall commit or authorize any act or omission by which the copyright of, or the right to copyright, this play may be impaired.

No one shall make any changes in this play for the purpose of production.

Publication of this play does not imply availability for performance. Both amateurs and professionals considering a production are strongly advised in their own interests to apply to Samuel French, Inc., for written permission before starting rehearsals, advertising, or booking a theatre.

No part of this book may be reproduced, stored in a retrieval system, or transmitted in any form, by any means, now known or yet to be invented, including mechanical, electronic, photocopying, recording, videotaping, or otherwise, without the prior written permission of the publisher.

IMPORTANT BILLING AND CREDIT REQUIREMENTS

All producers of *AMERICAN TALES* must give credit to the Authors of the Play in all programs distributed in connection with performances of the Play, and in all instances in which the title of the Play appears for the purposes of advertising, publicizing or otherwise exploiting the Play and /or a production. The name of the Authors *must* appear on a separate line on which no other name appears, immediately following the title and *must* appear in size of type not less than fifty percent of the size of the title type.

In addition the following credit *must* be given on the title page in the customary size and bottom page position of all programs distributed in association with LORT and/or commercial stage productions of this piece in the United States, Canada, or the United Kingdom:

Originally Produced by The Antaeus Company
John Apicella and Jeanie Hackett, Co-Artistic Directors
North Hollywood, California

AMERICAN TALES premiered at Deaf West Theatre in North Hollywood, California, on June 20th, 2008. The production was presented by The Antaeus Company and was directed by Kay Cole and Thor Steingraber, with the following cast:

ROSANNAH/GINGER NUT .... Devon Sorvari
ALONZO/NIPPERS .... Daniel Blinkoff
BURLEY/BARTLEBY .... Richard Miro / Raphael Sbarge
UNCLE CHARLES, MAID/TURKEY .... John Combs / Paul Eiding
DOCTOR/THE LAWYER .... Philip Proctor / Peter Van Norden

Melanie Lora (Cover) Rosannah/Ginger Nut

Orchestrations - Jan Powell
Musical Direction - Steven Ladd Jones and Billy Thompson
Scenic Design - Laura Fine Hawkes
Costumes - A. Jeffrey Schoenberg
Lighting Design - Jose Lopez
Sound Design - John Apicella
Props - Devin Gregory
Vocal Technique - Nancy Dussault and Marjorie Poe
Assistant Directors - Ben Durham and Jamie Wollrab
Alexander Technique - Jean-Louis Rodrique and Kristoff Konrad
Clowning Consultant - Orlando Pabotoy
Production Stage Manager - Young Ji
Stage Manager - Leia Crawford
Piano/Conductor - Michael Alfera and Steven Ladd Jones
Violin - Amanda Kopcsak
Bass - Jay Rubbottom
Producer - Laura Hill

THE LOVES OF ALONZO FITZ CLARENCE AND ROSANNAH ETHELTON

A one-act musical
from the story by Mark Twain

Book and Lyrics by　　　Music by
Ken Stone　　　　　　　Jan Powell

CAST OF CHARACTERS

ALONZO FITZ CLARENCE - a poetic soul, an idle young man transformed by true love into a tireless, steadfast lover

ROSANNAH ETHELTON - a lovely young woman of high spirits and high ideals

SIDNEY ALGERNON BURLEY - an unwelcome suitor to Rosannah, a born villain

DOCTOR - a compassionate man of middle age, owner of a private madhouse in New York

UNCLE CHARLES - uncle of Rosannah, middle-aged, missionary in Honolulu

MAID - *(doubled by "Uncle Charles")* an old and sour retainer at Rosannah's house

Doubling with Act II

ALONZO – NIPPERS
ROSANNAH – GINGER NUT
BURLEY – BARTLEBY
DOCTOR – LAWYER
UNCLE CHARLES – TURKEY

MUSICAL NUMBERS

Rosannah's Song	ROSANNAH
Rosannah's Song (*reprise*)	ROSANNAH, ALONZO
Ah, Lucky Maid!	BURLEY
Rosannah's Song (*reprise*)	ROSANNAH, ALONZO
A Rival	BURLEY
A Rival (*duet*)	ALONZO, BURLEY
The Faithful Traveler/My Love	ALL
O Happy Me	ROSANNAH
Onward!	ROSANNAH
Onward! (*reprise*)	ALL
Rosannah's Song (*reprise*)	ALONZO, ROSANNAH
My Love (*duet*)	ALONZO, ROSANNAH
Finale	ALL

SETTING

The 1890s, as imagined in the 1870s
Maine, California, New York, and the Sandwich Islands

Scene One

(The parlor of Alonzo Fitz Clarence in Eastport, Maine, early afternoon on a stormy winter day. **ALONZO**, *attired in his dressing gown, turns from the window.)*

ALONZO. What a storm is raging outside! That means no going out today. On so grim a day, one needs a new interest, a fresh element, to whet the dull edge of captivity. That was very neatly said, but it doesn't mean anything. One doesn't want the edge of captivity sharpened up, you know, but just the reverse. Or plainly stated, what to do for company?…But here is my answer, from the good hand of Alexander Graham Bell. I can pay a call on Aunt Susan and still enjoy the most perfect warmth and comfort. Then when the ravenous wind howls at my window, I shall laugh at him and say he merely sounds the death-cry of yesterday's world, a blighted world that did not know the telephone.

(Sitting down at his desk and speaking to it, or rather to a very early telephone apparatus that sits upon it.)

Aunt Susan!

(The voice of **ROSANNAH** *is heard, lifted in sentimental song, and* **ROSANNAH** *herself is seen, though some thousands of miles prevent* **ALONZO** *from sharing the view.)*

ROSANNAH.
WHEN YOU ARE NEAR, WHEN YOU ARE HERE,
AND I CAN GAZE AT YOUR FACE,
THE WORLD IS BRIGHT, THIS IS DELIGHT UNTOLD.

ALONZO. That is not Aunt Susan!

ROSANNAH.
I FEEL THE PRESS OF YOUR CARESS
IN EVERY HEARTFELT EMBRACE.
MY SPIRIT SOARS FOR I AM YOURS TO HOLD.

ALONZO. That is some angel!

ROSANNAH.
> HOW NEAR IS BLISS? AS NEAR AS THIS,
> AS NEAR AS TOUCHING YOUR FINGERS.
> THE WARMTH OF YOU LINGERS SO.
> POOR WORLD! WHAT CAN IT MAKE OF
> OUR JOY AS WE PARTAKE OF
> THE NEARNESS THAT LOVE ALONE CAN KNOW?

ALONZO. Oh angel, have you finished so soon?

ROSANNAH. You were not listening, sir?

ALONZO. When someone sings in my drawing room, why…I customarily do.

ROSANNAH. But I am in no such place, good sir.

ALONZO. And I the more wretched for that.

ROSANNAH. As we are not acquainted, I *could* be in no such place.

ALONZO. Let my Aunt Susan introduce us at once and the difficulty is removed.

ROSANNAH. That may do. Let us proceed.

ALONZO. Yes, let's.

(pause)

ROSANNAH. If she would be so good.

ALONZO. Oh, Aunt Susan is all goodness.

(pause)

ROSANNAH. Will you ask her, then?

ALONZO. I? Will you not?

ROSANNAH. Well, as she is *your* Aunt Susan, and as I have not had the pleasure of *her* acquaintance any more than your own –

ALONZO. Are you not visiting at her house? Have you not just now been singing in her downstairs parlor in Baltimore, Maryland?

ROSANNAH. Why…no. I am in my own home in San Francisco, California.

ALONZO. Then our meeting is by chance, and the kindest accident that ever fate devised.

ROSANNAH. Shall I understand that you are in Baltimore, sir?

ALONZO. I scarcely know anymore. Five minutes ago, confidently would I have answered that I was in the state of Maine on a dull and bitter cold afternoon, but now I fear my heart at least is in warm and shining California. Do tell me that you look out even now upon a bright, sunny afternoon.

ROSANNAH. I fear not.

ALONZO. Dash it!

ROSANNAH. But it is a bright, sunny *morning*, quarter past ten.

ALONZO. One thirty-two, and a heavy snow falling.

ROSANNAH. Then we have talked from morning to afternoon and still I do not know your name.

ALONZO. Wait a moment!

*(**ALONZO** rushes to throw off his dressing gown and put on his coat. When ready in his full dignity:)*

Mr. Alonzo Fitz Clarence of Eastport, Maine.

ROSANNAH. Miss Rosannah Ethelton, San Francisco, California.

ALONZO. I live here with my aged mother.

ROSANNAH. As do I. Just myself and dear old Mother.

ALONZO & ROSANNAH. And the servants.

ROSANNAH. But I am very content. At least I think I am. I knit, I sew, visit the poor, and write long letters to my uncle, a missionary to the heathen of Honolulu.

ALONZO. Whilst I, when Mother is not in need of my support and comfort, read books, take long walks through the town – sometimes indeed three quarters of a mile at a shot – and sometimes…dare I confess it?

ROSANNAH. What is it, Mr. Fitz Clarence?

ALONZO. No, I cannot. What *will* you think of me?

ROSANNAH. Is it so very bad?

ALONZO. Sometimes I…

ROSANNAH. Not drink, I hope!

ALONZO. Nay, worse. Sometimes…I write a line or two of poetry.

ROSANNAH. Why, you frightened me on purpose! How bad you are!

ALONZO. I cannot bear to hear you say so. Do forgive me, Miss Ethelton. Say that you will.

ROSANNAH. Perhaps. In time.

ALONZO. What have I but time? Time, the handmaiden of hope, that, like the last leaf of spring, never can turn to dross.

(modestly)

As the poet said.

ROSANNAH. I do not know that poet.

ALONZO. Will you sing again, Miss Ethelton?

ROSANNAH. Oh no, sir, I must go now. We have scarcely met and I must not overstay. Perhaps another day.

ALONZO. Tomorrow then!

ROSANNAH. Yes, perhaps. Perhaps tomorrow.

ALONZO. Until then let us have one more stanza. One measure. One note!

ROSANNAH. That is not sensible, Mr. Fitz Clarence. Let us say one minute.

ROSANNAH.	**ALONZO.**
WHEN YOU ARE NEAR, WHEN YOU ARE HERE, AND I CAN GAZE AT YOUR FACE,	OH, TO HEAR THAT VOICE AGAIN!
THE WORLD IS BRIGHT, THIS IS DELIGHT UNTOLD.	OH, BLESSED TELEPHONE! CAN IT BE? CAN IT LAST?
I FEEL THE PRESS OF YOUR CARESS IN EVERY HEARTFELT EMBRACE.	CAN I TRUST MY SENSES?
MY SPIRIT SOARS FOR I AM YOURS TO HOLD.	TO THINK I WAS LONELY!

ALONZO & ROSANNAH.
>HOW NEAR IS BLISS? AS NEAR AS THIS,
>AS NEAR AS TOUCHING YOUR FINGERS.
>THE WARMTH OF YOU LINGERS SO.
>POOR WORLD! WHAT CAN IT MAKE OF
>OUR JOY AS WE PARTAKE OF
>THE NEARNESS THAT LOVE ALONE CAN KNOW?

End of Scene

Scene Two

(Rosannah's parlor, San Francisco. **BURLEY** *is present, carrying a bouquet.)*

BURLEY.

A PERFECT DAY FOR COURTING,
FOR WINNING SOMEONE'S HEART,
A DAY FOR PRETTY FLATTERY,
THAT PROFITABLE ART.

(chucking his flowers under their little chins)

A DAY WHEN THINGS BOTANICAL
ARE FANCIED FOR THEIR POWER TO PERSUADE.

(He preens.)

AH, LUCKY MAID!

SHE'LL FIND I'M VERY CLEVER,
AND COUNTED EVEN WISE.
I'M RAVISHING TO LISTEN TO,
AND DAZZLING TO THE EYES.
MY ELOQUENCE WILL FLOW:
I'LL GIVE HER POEMS OR A LOVER'S SERENADE.
AH, LUCKY MAID!

IT'S POSSIBLE THAT SOME WOULD THINK I COURT
BENEATH MY STATION.
IT'S TRUE SHE HAS NO INTELLECT TO SPEAK OF.
HER SIZABLE INHERITANCE CAN BE MY
CONSOLATION,
FOR MONEY IS A PLEASANT THING TO REEK OF.

I'LL TEACH THE GIRL TO LOVE ME,
AND KEEP HER IN MY POW'R.
RESISTANCE, IF THERE'S ANY,
CANNOT LAST A QUARTER HOUR.
BY THEN, I DOUBT IT NOT,
SHE WILL HAVE GOT THE WORD FROM CUPID AND
OBEYED.
AH, LUCKY MAID!

ROSANNAH. *(entering, with no great pleasure at seeing* **BURLEY***)* Oh. Mr. Burley. I hope you didn't go to any trouble. What are those?

BURLEY. *(handing them over)* Why, they're…hyacinths or petunias or something. You know, flowers. Hothouse beauties acquired at great expense. But no more than you deserve, Miss Ethelton.

ROSANNAH. I'm sure I deserve nothing from you, Mr. Burley. Yet you've been so attentive lately.

BURLEY. No, no. Don't thank me.

ROSANNAH. Not in my wildest dreams.

BURLEY. Let me thank *you*. I was deeply honored to be invited to your soirée last evening.

ROSANNAH. Yes, Mother is so thoughtful.

BURLEY. And I hope you noticed I kept one or two people quite amused. I fear you couldn't hear me, for I didn't see you laughing.

ROSANNAH. Oh, I heard very well. It was good of you to entertain my guests with your vocal imitations. When you sang that song and quacked like a duck –

BURLEY. A popular song from the stage. (It was a goose in fact.)

ROSANNAH. And performed Lady Macbeth as your washerwoman might read the role –

BURLEY. That sort of thing is normally very welcome at parties.

ROSANNAH. Yes.

BURLEY. Shall I do another right now?

ROSANNAH. No.

BURLEY. Oh, have you heard the one –

ROSANNAH. Yes.

BURLEY. If somehow I have offended –

ROSANNAH. No, Mr. Burley. I'm afraid my mind…turns to other things. Thank you for calling.

BURLEY. Miss Ethelton, let me make it plain that I – that you – well, that I –

ROSANNAH. I must go back to my own little parlor now, Mr. Burley. But that was very plain. When I am in need of more plainness, I shall invite you back.

*(***ROSANNAH** *exits.* **BURLEY** *is thunderstruck, as if he might explode in anger. But no:)*

BURLEY. She loves me. By gad, she loves me! "I shall invite you back," says she. Yes indeed she will!

ALL RIGHT, THEN, NOT IN ONE DAY.
I'LL GLADLY GIVE IT TWO.
BUT NOTHING CAN DISCOURAGE ME
FROM WHAT I MEAN TO DO.
DELAY MAY CAUSE ME HURT,
BUT I AM CERTAIN TO BE HANDSOMELY REPAID
FOR HAVING STAYED.

AND WELL REPAID IS SHE
BY ACQUIRING HANDSOME ME.
SO A FORTUNE'S TO BE MADE,
AND A MAID IS TO BE FORTUNATE,
AND THAT, TO PUT IT CRUDELY, IS A TRADE.

(spoken)

Or more discreetly,
AH, LUCKY MAID!

End of Scene

Scene Three

(Rosannah's private sitting room and Alonzo's parlor. Rosannah's front door also visible. The action covers several weeks.)

ROSANNAH.
WHEN YOU ARE NEAR, WHEN YOU ARE HERE,
AND I CAN GAZE AT YOUR FACE,
THE WORLD IS BRIGHT, THIS IS DELIGHT UNTOLD.

Isn't it odd, Mr. Fitz Clarence? I know so many songs, yet I keep returning to that one.

ALONZO. Yes. Yes, so you do. But was ever song so sweet and so full of meaning?

ROSANNAH.
LA LA LA LA LA,
LA LA LA LA LA LA.

ALONZO. From the sound of your voice alone I know what I would see if you were here before me. The delicacy of your chin, those bright blue eyes, the ring of golden curls* round your brow...

ROSANNAH. *(examining the ends of her hair with some guilty insecurity)* Oh, I...why they...

ALONZO. When you sing, Miss Ethelton, I positively see you, as plainly as I see the clock upon the wall, telling four fifteen.

ROSANNAH. Twelve fifty-eight. Yes, it is perfectly true. With neither photograph nor sketch to guide me, I see you too, something over six feet in height, broad of shoulder, noble of countenance.

*(**ALONZO**, something of a dandy, usually has a mirror close at hand, and now makes use of one, but with some unease.)*

ALONZO. Well, as to that, as to height, as to six feet –

ROSANNAH. Forgive me, I should have said at least six feet *two* in boots. Your voice proclaims as much, Mr. Fitz Clarence. Is it not so?

---

* If the actress is blonde, Alonzo may say "ebony" curls.

ALONZO.
> LA LA LA LA LA,
> LA LA LA LA LA LA.

Such a dear old song.

*(Doorbell at **ROSANNAH**'s house. A very elderly **MAID** of sour disposition appears and opens the door to reveal **BURLEY**, holding another, larger bouquet.)*

BURLEY. Is Miss Ethelton at home?

MAID. What did I tell you yesterday?

BURLEY. A touch of dizziness, you said.

MAID. Gets worse every day.

(She starts to shut the door, then reopens it.)

Including tomorrow.

(She shuts the door in his face and exits.)

ALONZO. Let winter's tempest rage, I say, if only I be sheltered in the fire of those eyes.

ROSANNAH. Oh, poor Mr. Fitz Clarence. Is it still winter in Maine?

ALONZO. Still winter, save in those happy hours when we are talking.

*(Doorbell again. The **MAID** opens, **BURLEY** appears, equipped with an even larger bouquet.)*

BURLEY. Miss Ethelton is better today, I trust.

MAID. Can't say she is.

BURLEY. Then please do let me send my personal physician.

(She shuts the door in his face and exits.)

ROSANNAH. His name is Sidney Algernon Burley, and he's the most persistent, unwelcome creature. I wonder that we allow him in polite society. He appears now every day.

ALONZO. What effrontery, to call when he is unwanted. Oh, Miss Ethelton, you say true, do you not, that he is… unwanted?

ROSANNAH. My good Mr. Fitz Clarence, he is…unwanted.

ALONZO. Oh, happy day!

(Doorbell. The **MAID** *opens, sees* **BURLEY** *outside with an even larger bouquet, about to speak. She shuts the door in his face and exits.)*

ROSANNAH. Who can be as happy as I? And it is only your true and honest voice that has made me so.

ALONZO. My voice! Ah, but what is *my* voice compared to yours, Miss Ethelton, when you lift it in song and those golden** curls shimmer like waves upon the seashore of eternity…as the poet said.

(Doorbell. The **MAID** *opens.* **BURLEY** *steps forward, holding all his previous bouquets plus something that amounts almost to a potted tree, with which he prevents the* **MAID** *from closing the door.)*

BURLEY. *(loading her with the whole lot as he speaks sweetly)* There now, just you put these in water, you dear old thing. I'll see myself out.

(The **MAID** *sneers but stumbles out, fully loaded.* **BURLEY** *shuts the door, remaining within. When she is out of sight, he creeps to the closed door of Rosannah's sitting room and begins listening.)*

ROSANNAH. I marvel at the life I knew before, and was so foolish as to call happiness.

ALONZO. I too once deceived myself in that way.

BURLEY. *(aside)* A man? With her!

ROSANNAH. Imagine: I never have laid eyes on you, yet whenever we sing our own song together I feel I know you better than I know myself.

BURLEY. How's this? Never laid eyes on him?

ALONZO. Astonishing but true. In our age of marvels, one is paramount.

ROSANNAH. The word itself is almost sacred.

** Or ebony.

ALONZO. A very gift from the gods.

ROSANNAH. O telephone!

ALONZO. Telephone!

BURLEY. Telephone!

ALONZO. Distance is no more! Nothing again can separate two hearts bound by fervor, by *fevered* fervor, by fervid fever –

BURLEY. Oh, shut up!

ROSANNAH AND ALONZO. What did you say?

ALONZO. I? Why in one word, love, Rosannah. Love.

ROSANNAH. Love? Dare we employ that majestic word?

ALONZO. I for one shall dare. Before the heavens I proclaim it.

ROSANNAH. As do I, dearest Alonzo.

BURLEY. Curses!

> I HAVE A RIVAL
> WHO STAYS IN HIDING.
> HIS BLASTED TELEPHONE
> HAS MADE HER TOO CONFIDING.
> IT ISN'T DECENT.
> HE'S ALL TOO FREE THERE.
> AND MOST UNSUITABLE OF ALL
> IT ISN'T ME THERE.
> BETTER FAR IF A MAN OF NERVE
> HAD STOPPED HIM ERE HE BEGAN.
> I'LL LEARN HIS HIDEOUT,
> I'LL STORM THE PLACE,
> AND BRING THE MAN TO RUIN
> FACE TO FACE.

ROSANNAH. *(laughing)* I suppose I must expect another visit from Mr. Burley today. No matter, I know whom I love: Alonzo Fitz Clarence, Eastport, State of Maine.

BURLEY. Curse him, I've got his address, anyway! To Eastport, Maine, with all haste!

(A train whistle blows. Segue)

Scene Four

(On board a train. **BURLEY** *alone.)*

BURLEY.
MY HIDDEN RIVAL,
I WILL CONFRONT YOU.
I'LL MEET YOU MAN TO MAN AND FIGHT,
YOU LITTLE RUNT, YOU.
I WILL BE FORTHRIGHT.
I WILL BE CANDID.
OH NO I WON'T,
I'LL BE COMPLETELY UNDERHANDED.
MILE BY MILE, AS MY TRAIN SPEEDS ONWARD,
HOUR BY HOUR GROWS MY PLAN.
YOU'LL BE THE LOSER,
I'LL BE THE GROOM.
YES, I BRING A BITTER PILL,
WHICH I HOPE YOU WON'T TAKE ILL,
THOUGH I RATHER THINK YOU WILL:
YOUR DEFEAT, OR BETTER STILL
YOUR DOOM!

(Segue)

Scene Five

*(**ALONZO**'s parlor in Eastport, Maine. **BURLEY**, in the doorway, addresses **ALONZO**.)*

BURLEY. Mr. Fitz Clarence?

ALONZO. Yes, sir, so I am.

BURLEY. My card.

ALONZO. "Professor Claudius Beaupré, inventor." Well, sir, what have you invented?

BURLEY. An improvement in ze téléphone.

(He flourishes a large suitcase adorned with a French flag.)

ALONZO. *(proudly)* Mettez – la – valise – sur – la – chaise.

(beat)

BURLEY. Thank you no, I never touch a drop. May I put my suitcase on your chair?

ALONZO. Yes, of course.

BURLEY. You may not know that a man today may go and tap a telegraph wire that carry a song, a concert, from one state to another. He attach his private telephone, he steal a hearing of that music as it pass along. My invention will stop all that.

ALONZO. Well, if the owner of the music could not miss what was stolen, why should he care?

BURLEY. Ah, but now suppose the wire, he carry not the music, he carry the love talking, kiss-kiss.

ALONZO. Sir, it is a priceless invention! I must have it at any cost.

BURLEY. You are so lucky; I have one apparatus remaining. I set to work at once.

*(**BURLEY** goes to the telephone. **ALONZO** watches. As **BURLEY** grows more frustrated, his accent increasingly wavers.)*

Have you got a crosscut saw?

ALONZO. Certainly. In the next room.

BURLEY. Forty-five feet of copper wire?

ALONZO. Oh yes, Cook can turn up anything in the kitchen.

BURLEY. Ivory-handled tin snips.

ALONZO. I'll go get Mother's.

BURLEY. Five brass buttons from the uniform of a British admiral.

ALONZO. Well, I'll have to rummage about for that.

BURLEY. Very good. Take your time.

*(**ALONZO** leaves. **BURLEY** listens to him depart, waits a moment, then:)*

(imitating Alonzo's voice) Sweetheart?

ROSANNAH. Yes, Alonzo?

BURLEY. Will you sing today?

ROSANNAH. Only too gladly, my dearest. Our own sweet song.

BURLEY. No, please don't sing *that* anymore this week. Try something modern.

ALONZO. *(approaching from outside the room)* Professor Beaupré!

*(**BURLEY** swiftly disappears behind a curtain. **ALONZO** enters.)*

Will three silver cufflinks do as well? Why, where has he gone?

ROSANNAH. *(icily)* Do as well as what?

ALONZO. Rosannah, dear! Shall we sing something together today?

ROSANNAH. Something modern?

ALONZO. Yes, if you prefer.

ROSANNAH. Sing it yourself!

ALONZO. Rosannah, that was not like you.

ROSANNAH. I suppose it becomes me as much as your very polite speech became you, Mr. Fitz Clarence.

ALONZO. Mr. Fitz Clarence! Rosannah, there was nothing impolite about my speech.

ROSANNAH. Oh, indeed! Of course, then, I misunderstood you, and I most humbly beg your pardon, ha-ha-ha! No doubt you said, "Please sing it again."

ALONZO. Sing what again?

ROSANNAH. The song you mentioned, of course. How very obtuse we are, all of a sudden!

ALONZO. I never mentioned any song.

ROSANNAH. Oh, you didn't?

ALONZO. No, I didn't!

ROSANNAH. Perhaps the telephone spoke without your knowledge?

ALONZO. Yes! That must be it.

ROSANNAH. That is sufficient, sir. I will never forgive you. All is over between us.

(She sobs away into the distance.)

ALONZO. Oh, Rosannah, unsay those words!

(no answer)

There is some dreadful mystery here, some hideous mistake. I must find Professor Beaupré and have the telephone regulated!

*(**ALONZO** rushes out. **BURLEY** emerges, full of confidence and villainy as he approaches the telephone.)*

BURLEY. Her womanly heart may hold to that resolution for ten seconds, but not one instant longer. Eight, nine, ten.

ROSANNAH. Alonzo, dear, I have been wrong. You could not have said so cruel a thing. Let us believe, for love's sake, that the telephone is to blame.

BURLEY. *(as **ALONZO**)* You have said all was over between us. So let it be. I spurn your proffered repentance, and despise it!

*(**BURLEY** dashes out of the house; **ALONZO** reenters, in time to hear **ROSANNAH**:)*

ROSANNAH. Then goodbye, Mr. Fitz Clarence, formerly my Alonzo. Do not attempt to find me. I nevermore will be seen in my familiar haunts. I renounce this life and all its vanity. I go to wander friendless through the world.

(She is gone.)

ALONZO. No! Dear heart, no! Rosannah? Rosannah? Gone! This never can be. I leave at once for San Francisco, there to search from palace to hovel until she is found.

(He sees the apparatus before him.)

But hold, my telephone apparatus shall be my ace. If it be true that one can listen to sounds as they pass over the wire, then I must follow that wire over every telegraph pole from Maine to California. One day she will sing that dear song again, and I, atop some helpful pole, shall hear.

(He picks up a card that has fallen to the floor.)

"Mr. Sidney Algernon Burley, San Francisco." What? The unwanted suitor of my Rosannah! This was he then, no inventor. And some foul words of his have hardened my darling's heart against me!

I HAVE A RIVAL.
OH, EVIL SCHEMER.
IF YOU WERE HERE AGAIN,
I'D KICK YOU IN THE FEMUR.

BURLEY. *(appearing elsewhere)*

MY FORMER RIVAL,
YOU FEEL A COMEDOWN,
LIKE ANY MAGGOT FEELS
WHEN BURLEY PUTS HIS THUMB DOWN.

ALONZO.

WHEN HAS MAN BEEN SO VILE A MONSTER?

BURLEY.

WELL, ONE DOES WHAT ONE CAN.
I'D LIKE MY BATH NOW.

ALONZO.

I'D LIKE TO FIGHT.
I WOULD FACE THE FIENDS OF HELL
TO PUT THINGS RIGHT.

(Change of scene begins. **ALONZO** *is packing up and leaving home.* **BURLEY** *is in his bath.)*

ALONZO *(cont.)*
> OH, CURSED RIVAL!
> THIS IS YOUR DOING!

BURLEY.
> SHE WILL BE MINE
> WHEN SHE IS DONE WITH HER BOOHOOING.

ALONZO.
> I'M BUT A NOMAD,
> CONDEMNED TO WANDER.

BURLEY.
> I THINK I'D LIKE IT
> IF HER HAIR WERE SOMEWHAT BLONDER.

ALONZO & BURLEY. *(In the case of* **BURLEY** *this is a happy reference to self.)*
> NEVER, NEVER HAS ONE SO FAIR
> BEEN FOOLED BY SO FOUL A MAN.

ALONZO.
> I'M FEELING WRETCHED.

BURLEY.
> I'M FEELING FINE.

ALONZO.
> LET HIM ROT, FOR ALL I CARE.

BURLEY.
> STILL, IT'S DAMNED ATTRACTIVE HAIR.

ALONZO.
> I'D LAY HANDS ON HIM, I SWEAR.

BURLEY.
> AND HER FORTUNE'S RATHER RARE.

ALONZO & BURLEY.
> NO EXERTION WILL I SPARE
> TILL THE DAY I CAN DECLARE
> SHE'S MINE.

End of Scene

Scene Six

(The open road. **ALONZO** *is a foot traveler, transporting among other things a portable telephone apparatus. A* **QUARTET** *presents itself.)*

QUARTET.

THROUGH WIND AND RAIN AND LIGHTNING CRASHING,
THROUGH DARK OF NIGHT AND HEAT OF DAY,
ALL FRIENDLESS DID THE MAN PRESS ONWARD,
ALL HOPEFUL DID HE MAKE HIS WAY.

*(***ALONZO*** throughout the scene is walking, stopping to deploy his telephone, failing to find what he seeks, repacking and walking again. Perhaps he takes out a map, studies then discards it, clearly lost and trusting to fate, not to a plan. Perhaps the* **QUARTET**, *carrying cutouts of telegraph poles, file in endless procession past his bewildered but far-seeing eyes. Perhaps too each has an element with which to assault him: dirt from a pail, rain from a watering can, snow from a sieve, wind from a bellows.)*

QUARTET. *(cont.)*

WHEN NIGHT WOULD FALL, HE SCOFFED AT SHELTER.
FOR SHELTER HE HAD THOUGHTS OF LOVE.
FOR FOOD AND DRINK HE HAD SWEET MEM'RY.
FOR THESE HE THANKED THE STARS ABOVE.

OH, YOU FAITHFUL TRAVELER,
OH, BE FAITHFUL STILL.
THE TIME WILL COME WHEN LOVE'S REQUITED.
THE TIME WILL COME, I SWEAR IT WILL.

ALONZO.

MY LOVE'S A GLOWING CANDLE IN THE DARKEST NIGHT,
THE LIGHT BY WHICH MY WORLD ITSELF IS KNOWN.
WHO AM I TO FEAR THE DARKNESS?
WHO AM I TO FEEL ALONE?

ALONZO. *(cont.)*
> MY LOVE'S A VOICE UNDAUNTED BY TEN THOUSAND MILES,
> THAT KNOWS BOTH HOW TO SUMMON AND SUSTAIN.
> WHO AM I TO THINK OF HUNGER?
> WHO AM I TO SPEAK OF PAIN?
>
> YET I COULD SEARCH FOR A SCORE OF YEARS
> AND LOSE HER EVEN SO.
> WILL MY EARTHLY STRENGTH PASS AWAY TOO SOON?
> NO, IT'S BETTER NOT TO KNOW.
>
> MY LOVE IS MY SALVATION AND MY CROWN OF THORNS,
> ONE BEACON IN MY LIFE, FOREVER TRUE.
> I'M A MAN, A MAN WHO LOVES HER.
> I'M A MAN BECAUSE I DO.

(The scene begins to change.)

QUARTET.
> A NOBLE HEART ENDURES FOREVER,
> BUT FLESH IS WEAK AND FEET GROW SORE.
> ONE DAY IN FRESNO, CALIFORNIA,

*(They point **ALONZO** toward Fresno, California, offstage, and he goes.)*

> THE TRAVELER, HE COULD WALK NO MORE.

(The offstage sound of a collapsing traveler.)

> OH, YOU FAITHFUL TRAVELER,
> OH, BE FAITHFUL STILL.
> THE TIME WILL COME WHEN LOVE'S REQUITED.
> THE TIME WILL COME, I SWEAR IT WILL.

*(Exit **QUARTET** except **ROSANNAH**, who remains and becomes herself again. Segue)*

Scene Seven

(**ROSANNAH** *in limbo.*)

ROSANNAH. *(Her manner not nearly as convincing as her words.)*
FREE! NOW I AM FREE, ERGO I'M HAPPY.
SEE HOW I CAN SMILE AT THE TROUBLES BEHIND.
SAFE, KNOWING THAT NOTHING MORE CAN TOUCH ME.
THE PATH INTO MY SOUL NONE SHALL FIND NOW.

HEART FIRMLY UNPLIGHTED, TELEPHONE UNWIRED,
PROOF AM I AGAINST ALL PAIN.
HERE STAND I ALONE, HERE STAY I FOREVER,
EXQUISITELY FREE. O HAPPY ME.

(The location is revealed as Fresno, California, the Open-Door Salvation Mission for destitute heathen. **ROSANNAH** *is inside,* **ALONZO** *approaches the door.)*

ALONZO. *(reading)* "The Open-Door Salvation Mission. Tired travelers, souls in distress, repentant pirates, et cetera. Welcome all." What kindly hand has written such words upon a shingle in Fresno, California? I will inquire.

ROSANNAH. Good evening, sir.

ALONZO. Your sign, miss, caught my eye.

ROSANNAH. You are not, I suppose, a repentant pirate?

ALONZO. Why no. Do you get many?

ROSANNAH. Not one yet.

ALONZO. I am, however, a tired traveler.

ROSANNAH. That will do, sir, so long as I can be of service to one in need. Let our mission offer you food and rest.

(They enter.)

ALONZO. Your kindness, no less than your food, will give me strength for another day's quest. But what shall I call you, if "angel of mercy" be too effusive for convenient use?

ROSANNAH. I am…Miss Smith.

ALONZO. How kind you are, Miss Smith. And I am one in need of kindness.

ROSANNAH. Have you traveled very far?

ALONZO. Far indeed. From the state of Maine.

ROSANNAH. *(with a pang)* I have heard of such a place.

ALONZO. And little mercy was I shown along the way, Miss Smith, as these bullet holes in my clothing may attest.

ROSANNAH. How very horrid, sir.

ALONZO. Often when I was atop a telegraph pole – where I had good and noble cause to be, I assure you –

ROSANNAH. Oh, yes.

ALONZO. – neighbor and stranger alike would shoot guns at me, and abuse me with such words as, "This'll take your feathers off, ye blasted crow!" thinking me mad, I suppose.

ROSANNAH. How dreadful that your erstwhile friends could use you so ill, Mr. Crowe. But you have come now to a better place, where I hope kindness may be shown to all. Let me bring you something to eat.

(He sits at a table. She begins to work, while softly and sadly singing to herself.)

WHEN YOU ARE NEAR, WHEN YOU ARE HERE,
AND I CAN GAZE AT YOUR FACE,
THE WORLD IS BRIGHT, THIS IS DELIGHT UNTOLD.
I FEEL THE PRESS OF YOUR CARESS
IN EVERY HEARTFELT EMBRACE.
MY SPIRIT SOARS FOR I AM YOURS TO HOLD.

*(**ALONZO** is transfixed by the sound, and stumbles to his feet. As she returns to the table with food, she sees the look on his face and nearly screams.)*

Oh! Have I disturbed you?

(Music continues underneath, a solo violin, so to speak.)

ALONZO. No, no, you just put me in mind of someone who used to sing that song.

ROSANNAH. Who, Mr. Crowe?

ALONZO. Oh, someone who…

(He looks, but gives up, shaking his head.)

…looks nothing like you. Forgive me; my mind grows weak. I am like a clock run dry, a vessel wracked upon the precipice of despair. As the poet said.

ROSANNAH. I do not know that poet.

ALONZO. Three thousand miles of walking do things to a man.

ROSANNAH. *(Beginning to take on a tone we have not heard before. She has the makings of a preacher in her – or a passionate lover.)* Poor, heartbroken man. But surely your great cause, whatever it may be, does not die because your shoe leather is worn through. Surely if a thousand miles more may bring you to your destination, you will not falter now. Surely if a mere stranger like myself can read in your eye the power to be victorious, think how those who know and love you must expect from you great things. Great things, born of great, great perseverance…Mr. Crowe.

(Her breast is heaving, and but for those regrettable last two words he might have taken her in his arms. But he moves away now, and eyes the horizon. A march begins.)

ALONZO. You are right, Miss Smith. If I can cross the country once, I can cross it ten times. Providence would not bring me this far only to mock me in my quest. I feel a higher power watching over me, Miss Smith, thanks to your kind words. If I in turn had words to express my gratitude –

ROSANNAH. No, sir, no. Can you not see what you have given me? To have been the poor instrument that set a wanderer back upon his true course. What joy! I see my own path before me now, for the first time. I believe I have the calling and the gift.

(picking up her suitcase)

I shall journey to the Sandwich Islands, and there join my aged uncle as a missionary to the heathen of Honolulu.

ALONZO. What?!

(He stops for long cogitation.)

How frequently one hears that these days. It reflects so well upon our enlightened age. Bon voyage, Miss Smith.

ROSANNAH.

ONWARD! THE WORLD AWAITS AND CALLS US FORTH,
SO ONWARD! IT'S HERE THE JOURNEY STARTS.
FORWARD! THOUGH PAIN AND STRIFE MAY LIE AHEAD,
CRY FORWARD! WITH COURAGE IN OUR HEARTS.
UPWARD! AS EVERY NOBLE MIND DESIRES.
YES, UPWARD! WHERE HOPES AND PRAYERS ASCEND,
UNTIL THE SOUND OF THE FINAL TRUMPET CALL,
WHEN IT'S HEAVENWARD TO JOURNEY'S END.

*(**ROSANNAH** marches off. **ALONZO** sighs after her, then comes to his senses and at last falls ravenously to eating. A **PIRATE** appears at the window.)*

BURLEY. *(...for **BURLEY** it is)* Can I be too late? It is he!

*(to **ALONZO**)*

Is there a young lady here who saves the wicked?

ALONZO. Great heavens, a pirate in Fresno, California?

BURLEY. But I'm repentant.

ALONZO. Exactly. And after all her waiting she's only just missed you.

BURLEY. Is she gone?

ALONZO. Gone, yes, but you can find her in Honolulu. Hurry, sir, and when you find her, do not fail to ask for her beef stew. As for me, I'm resuming my search for true love, wherever it may lead me!

(exit)

BURLEY. *(de-pirating)* Godspeed, Mr. Fitz Clarence, you fool. And since you insist, I shall be delighted to visit the islands.

End of Scene

Scene Eight

(The open road once again. **ALONZO** *alone.)*

ALONZO. Now, which way? North to San Francisco?

*(***ALONZO** *is at* **ROSANNAH***'s house. The* **MAID** *opens.)*

Alonzo Fitz Clarence.

MAID. You scoundrel! Here? And my mistress out wandering the cold, cruel world –

*(***ALONZO** *shuts the door.)*

ALONZO. She is not at home then. But if she has quitted San Francisco, where would she go? Can there be any hope of finding her? Yes. For when I falter, I hear the voice of my Rosannah saying

ROSANNAH. *(entering, dressed as an angel, as* **ALONZO** *lipsyncs)* Follow the telegraph wire. I am here.

ALONZO. And when I stumble, I hear her say

BURLEY. *(entering, dressed as a devil)* Die in a ditch.

ALONZO. No, no. That is not my darling, but another's voice. And yet, it too has a power over me. Oh, friendly ditch.

BURLEY. Yes, you idiot. You have lost her.

ROSANNAH. No, while there is still a telegraph wire to follow, hope remains.

ALONZO. Yes, but which wire?

BURLEY. Give up, you fool.

ALONZO. Which ditch?

ROSANNAH. Never despair.

ALONZO. No, I never can.

BURLEY. Jump off a cliff.

ALONZO. Oh, gladly, gladly.

(a revelation)

I am losing my mind!

ROSANNAH.
ONWARD! THE WORLD AWAITS AND CALLS US FORTH,
SO ONWARD! IT'S HERE THE JOURNEY STARTS.

ALONZO. And now when I most need my Rosannah, it is the voice of Miss Smith that I hear. This is too cruel!
BURLEY. You blubbering disgrace to manhood.
ROSANNAH. Aw, leave the poor kid alone, why don't you?
BURLEY. Oh dear, how sentimental we are!

*(During the following, **ROSANNAH** and **BURLEY** focus their fury at each other, disregarding **ALONZO**. Before long they are ripping off each other's wings, halo, horns, etc., which greatly interferes with their singing. **ALONZO**, seeing he has been forgotten, looks askance at them and trudges onward, beyond hope, beyond despair, merely walking.)*

ROSANNAH.	BURLEY.	ALONZO.
ONWARD! THE WORLD AWAITS AND CALLS US FORTH, SO ONWARD! IT'S HERE THE JOURNEY STARTS.	THIS COULD BE MEXICO OR ZANZIBAR FOR ALL HE KNOWS. A VERY FOOL OF FOOLS, AN EMPTY VESSEL.	
FORWARD! THOUGH PAIN AND STRIFE MAY LIE AHEAD,	YOU SHOW YOUR CLAWS TO ME? I DIDN'T FEEL THAT.	Sacramento? Boise?
CRY FORWARD! WITH COURAGE IN OUR HEARTS.	I LAUGH, HA, HA! I LAUGH, HA, HA! ALL RIGHT THEN, NOW YOU'VE GONE AND DONE IT.	Phoenix? Albuquerque?
UPWARD! AS EVERY NOBLE MIND DESIRES.	I'M GOING TO THROTTLE YOU. I'M GOING TO THRASH YOU.	Denver? Austin?

ROSANNAH.	BURLEY.	ALONZO.
YES, UPWARD!	AND YOU	Tulsa?
WHERE HOPES AND PRAYERS ASCEND,	DESERVE IT FOR ENCOURAGING THE DOLT.	Madison?
UNTIL THE SOUND OF THE FINAL TRUMPET CALL,	IS THAT ENOUGH NOW? SHALL I GET ROUGH NOW?	Louisville? Chattanooga?
	YOU'VE THROWN YOUR LITTLE FIT,	Charleston? Pittsburgh?
WHEN IT'S HEAVENWARD TO JOURNEY'S,	BUT HERE'S AN END TO IT.	
HEAVENWARD TO JOURNEY'S –	NOW, NOW, YOU NEEDN'T HIT!	

(A light as from heaven strikes **ALONZO**. *He freezes, as do* **ROSANNAH** *and* **BURLEY**, *who are now in complete disarray.)*

DOCTOR AND UNCLE CHARLES.
AH! AH!

ALONZO. *(eyeing the horizon)* What bright city now lies before me? It is the great metropolis we call New York. Where indeed will I find more converging telegraph wires than here? Perhaps…perhaps…perhaps…

(He steps forward.)

ROSANNAH. *(Tattered but striving for dignity, she puts before* **ALONZO** *a respectable New York doorstep.)* Oh, true heart, see the good and solid shelter that stands before you. You are saved.

BURLEY. *(Hanging on the door a sign reading "Asylum.")* In short, welcome to the madhouse!

*(***ROSANNAH** *and* **BURLEY** *exit. Segue.)*

Scene Nine

(A private asylum in New York. **ALONZO** *stumbles to its doorstep, pulls the bell, and there collapses.)*

DOCTOR. *(answering the door)* Why, young man, are you ill?

ALONZO. *(delirious)* Rosannah. Oh, Rosannah.

DOCTOR. Ah, the poor fellow murmurs the name of his sainted mother. By what grace of providence did his collapse occur on the very steps of a mental asylum? Come, my good man, I am a doctor.

*(***ALONZO*** is helped inside by the* **DOCTOR.***)*

Sit here a moment in my private office. We'll soon see what to do with you.

(on the telephone)

Just bringing in a new patient, Charles. Well, I won't deny that I envy you sometimes. To bring help to the needy as you do, but in so fine a climate. How different from what we knew as boys together here in New York. And yet, you and I have lived to see the day when we can speak to each other as if in the same room. What times we do live in!

ROSANNAH. *(a disembodied voice)*
WHEN YOU ARE NEAR, WHEN YOU ARE HERE,
AND I CAN GAZE AT YOUR FACE,
THE WORLD IS BRIGHT, THIS IS DELIGHT UNTOLD.

(At the sound, **ALONZO** *stirs.)*

ALONZO. Can it be? This is a miracle!

DOCTOR. Yes, you may not have seen one of these. It's a telephone.

ALONZO. Great heavens, at last!

DOCTOR. You take an interest in new inventions? That's an excellent sign.

ALONZO. Rosannah! Rosannah!

DOCTOR. Now, my poor fellow, your mother is no more. Even the telephone can't reach beyond the grave.

ALONZO. Speak to me, Rosannah! It is Alonzo! The cruel mystery has been unraveled: It was the villain Burley who mimicked my voice and wounded you with insolent speech!

DOCTOR. Charles, my new patient is somewhat confused by the phenomenon of telephony. Let us talk tomorrow.

*(*ROSANNAH *and* UNCLE CHARLES *appear, in limbo.)*

ROSANNAH. Alonzo? My own Alonzo?

DOCTOR. Great Scott! Charles, you are not conducting a séance, I hope.

UNCLE CHARLES. No, this is my niece you are hearing, my Rosannah.

ALONZO. Rosannah! Rosannah darling, where are you?

ROSANNAH. Honolulu, Sandwich Islands. I assist my Uncle Charles, the missionary.

ALONZO. No!

(upon reflection:)

But yes, I would expect no less of you. Say, I don't suppose you know Miss Smith?

ROSANNAH. I don't think so. Why?

ALONZO. No matter. Nothing else matters now. Let us name the day.

ROSANNAH. Why, the very day you arrive in Honolulu.

DOCTOR. This man is not at all fit for travel.

ROSANNAH. Not ill, my Alonzo?

ALONZO. No, no, no, no. Somewhat fatigued, perhaps. I have walked twice across North America. I would not refuse a warm bed.

DOCTOR. Complete bed rest and a thorough mental examination.

ROSANNAH. But our wedding! How are we to be married?

ALONZO. My own dear heart, you know the answer.

HOW NEAR IS BLISS? AS NEAR AS THIS,

ROSANNAH.

AS NEAR AS TOUCHING YOUR FINGERS.

ALONZO.
THE WARMTH OF YOU LINGERS SO.
ALONZO & ROSANNAH.
POOR WORLD! WHAT CAN IT MAKE OF
OUR JOY AS WE PARTAKE OF
THE NEARNESS THAT LOVE ALONE CAN KNOW?

(**ALONZO** *is bundled off by the* **DOCTOR**. *We focus on Honolulu. Segue*)

Scene Ten

(A front porch in Honolulu, where **UNCLE CHARLES**, *regrettably, is learning to play the ukulele.* **BURLEY** *appears, presents his card, and withdraws to preen.)*

UNCLE CHARLES. A visitor for you, my dear. A Mr. Burley of San Francisco.

ROSANNAH. *(peeking outside)* Mr. Burley! Here!

UNCLE CHARLES. Shall I send him away?

ROSANNAH. *(fury contained, but barely)* Why Uncle, that would be very unchristian. Let him speak to me…if he dares.

*(***ROSANNAH** *confronts* **BURLEY**. **UNCLE CHARLES** *lingers, playing the ukulele.* **BURLEY** *tries hard to ignore it.)*

BURLEY. Miss Ethelton! It is true. It is you. At long last I have the very great pleasure of seeing you again.

ROSANNAH. Well?

BURLEY. To stand before you in such a place of abundant beauty, of nature's perfection, a place, may one say, of romance.

ROSANNAH. Well?

BURLEY. How are you?

ROSANNAH. Well.

BURLEY. I have been distressed beyond words at your…disappearance. I followed, I searched.

ROSANNAH. I was cruelly used, sir.

BURLEY. How it pains me to hear that. I would do anything to relieve your suffering.

ROSANNAH. How kind.

BURLEY. Only name it.

ROSANNAH. Well, Mr. Burley, one who deceived me in love has been unmasked, and I am free, indeed eager, to marry another.

BURLEY. Another?

ROSANNAH. Have you a top hat?

BURLEY. A very fine one.

ROSANNAH. Wear it on Saturday and be here at nine a.m. The ceremony must not begin late.

BURLEY. Oh, Miss Ethelton –

ROSANNAH. Until then I have not another word to say.

BURLEY. You have made me the happiest of men.

ROSANNAH. But that is nothing as compared to what you will feel on Saturday.

End of Scene

Scene Eleven

(Honolulu and New York. **UNCLE CHARLES** *in the former location, the* **DOCTOR** *in the latter.)*

UNCLE CHARLES. Herbert, I trust the honeymoon preparations are complete on your side.

DOCTOR. Everything done. And you?

UNCLE CHARLES. Couldn't be better.

*(***ROSANNAH** *enters.)*

Here is the bride now, and very beautiful, I assure you.

*(***ALONZO** *enters.)*

DOCTOR. The groom will do very well too, I see.

*(***BURLEY** *enters, overdressed in formalwear, out of place next to the others, and hot.)*

UNCLE CHARLES. Just in time, Mr. Burley. You may stand here. We are complete then. Well. Dearly beloved, we are gathered here today – and not, as the case may be – to consecrate the union of Rosannah Ethelton and Alonzo Fitz Clarence.

BURLEY. Sir! What does this mean?

UNCLE CHARLES. Pardon me, I should add: in the presence of the witness, Mr. Sidney Algernon Burley.

BURLEY. The witness? The witness? Bridegroom, you mean.

UNCLE CHARLES. Oh, we already have one of those, haven't we, Rosannah?

ROSANNAH. Yes, Uncle, indeed we have.

BURLEY. Let the coward show himself.

ALONZO. I can't quite manage that at present, Professor Beaupré.

BURLEY. The cursed telephone again!

ROSANNAH. If you cannot be quiet, Mr. Burley –

BURLEY. No, I cannot be quiet! I am betrayed! I am mocked! Here I stand before her, a man of substance and…substance! and she passes me over in favor of, of…

ROSANNAH. Mr. Burley, I pass you over because you are contemptible.

BURLEY. That is not to the point. Very well, all of you, I see my mistake, and never again will I make it. A solemn oath do I swear, and call you to witness: Before another sun sets, I too will be the owner of a telephone!

(exit)

UNCLE CHARLES. I believe we can resume. Alonzo, do you take this…voice?

ALONZO.
MY LOVE'S A SONG THAT FOLLOWS ME THROUGH EVERY DAY,
MORE REAL TO ME THAN SOLID FLESH AND BONE.
NEVERMORE WILL I KNOW SILENCE.
NEVERMORE ONE HEART ALONE.

ROSANNAH.
MY LOVE'S A VOICE THAT REACHES EVERY HIDDEN PLACE,
A VOICE TO WHICH NO SECRET IS UNKNOWN.
NEVERMORE WILL I KNOW SILENCE.
NEVERMORE ONE HEART ALONE.

ALONZO & ROSANNAH.
YOU ARE NEAR TO ME AS BREATHING,
THOUGH YOU WALK A DISTANT SHORE.
YOU ARE PART OF ME FOREVER,
NOW THAT DISTANCE IS NO MORE.

UNCLE CHARLES. I now pronounce you man and wife. You may kiss the bride should that opportunity ever present itself.

(The newlyweds are glowing with happiness.)

ALONZO. Rosannah darling, I hope you have a splendid honeymoon.

ROSANNAH. Oh, Alonzo dearest, I wish you the best honeymoon ever.

ALONZO. Farewell, then.

ROSANNAH. We will speak soon.

ALONZO. Very soon, my love. But now, my train awaits. Or rather, it does not await. It departs. A half hour from now, at two thirty-seven.

ROSANNAH. Nine fifty-one. And my ship sails at noon. Goodbye for now, my dear.

ALONZO. Goodbye, but only until the next telephone.

(ALONZO & ROSANNAH exit.)

UNCLE CHARLES. Herbert, you *are* certain I have not just married my niece to a lunatic?

DOCTOR. On examination he proved as sane as…well, as the world we live in. The story of his travels was unique in my experience, but no fantasy. We proved that, when your Rosannah told you of the episode that corresponded exactly to one her young man told me.

UNCLE CHARLES. Fortunately we are old and foolish, and therefore understood its meaning.

DOCTOR. Fortunately we are old and foolish, and therefore know that some things are better done without the assistance of Alexander Graham Bell!

UNCLE CHARLES. Such as honeymoons.

(Separately, the lovers: **ROSANNAH** *on board ship,* **ALONZO** *on a train, both pensive at best: This is not just precisely as much fun as they foresaw.)*

ROSANNAH.
WHEN YOU ARE NEAR, WHEN YOU ARE HERE,
AND I CAN GAZE AT YOUR FACE,
THE WORLD IS BRIGHT, THIS IS DELIGHT UNTOLD.

ALONZO.
I FEEL THE PRESS OF YOUR CARESS
IN EVERY HEARTFELT EMBRACE.
MY SPIRIT SOARS FOR I AM YOURS TO HOLD.

(They both look…is it possible? lonely.)

UNCLE CHARLES. How surprised she will be that her ship is not touring the islands but steaming for San Francisco.

DOCTOR. How surprised he will be when his train bypasses Niagara Falls and takes him due west.

UNCLE CHARLES. And whatever will they both think on finding a final train ticket in a sealed envelope with an appointment for ten days hence,

DOCTOR. Two thirty p.m.,

UNCLE CHARLES. At the Open-Door Salvation Mission,

UNCLE CHARLES AND DOCTOR. Fresno, California.

*(****ALONZO & ROSANNAH****, in Fresno, see and recognize each other and touch at last.)*

COMPANY
HOW NEAR IS BLISS? AS NEAR AS THIS,
AS NEAR AS TOUCHING YOUR FINGERS.
THE WARMTH OF YOU LINGERS SO.
POOR WORLD! WHAT CAN IT MAKE OF
OUR JOY AS WE PARTAKE OF
THE NEARNESS THAT LOVE ALONE CAN KNOW?

The End

BARTLEBY, THE SCRIVENER

A one-act musical
from the story by Herman Melville

Book and Lyrics by **Music by**
Ken Stone **Jan Powell**

CAST OF CHARACTERS

THE LAWYER - 55, affluent and self-satisfied

BARTLEBY - a fairly young man, enigmatic, turned almost entirely in upon himself

TURKEY - clerk, an Englishman near 60, something of a drinker

NIPPERS - clerk about 25, high-strung and restless

GINGER NUT - 12, law student, errand boy, sweeper, most often a brat

Doubling with Act I

LAWYER – DOCTOR
BARTLEBY – BURLEY
TURKEY – UNCLE CHARLES
NIPPERS – ALONZO
GINGER NUT – ROSANNAH

MUSICAL NUMBERS

A Snug Little Practice .... **THE LAWYER**
A Snug Little Practice (*reprise*) .... **TURKEY, NIPPERS, GINGER NUT**
This Can't Go On .... **TURKEY, NIPPERS, GINGER NUT**
The Wall .... **BARTLEBY**
I Would Prefer Not To .... **THE LAWYER, BARTLEBY**
Fare You Well .... **THE LAWYER, TURKEY, NIPPERS, GINGER NUT**
You Must Begone .... **THE LAWYER**
The Debt .... **THE LAWYER**
A Very Fine Place to Be Young .... **THE LAWYER**
Finale .... **BARTLEBY, THE LAWYER**

SETTING

New York, the 1840s

Scene One

*(A law office in New York, the 1840s. Simply furnished. High stools at large writing tables. Ink, pens, and an abundance of papers. Two men, **TURKEY** and **NIPPERS**, bend over their work.)*

*(A doorbell rings, and in answer, **THE LAWYER** enters. He is a successful man well into middle age, sure of his own worth but plain and direct in his manner, and more than a little proud of his humility.)*

THE LAWYER. *(narrating)* There are other lawyers in my position who would disdain to answer their own door, but I hold that putting on airs only hinders the doing of a good day's work.

*(**THE LAWYER** opens the door. Outside stands **BARTLEBY**, a young man with something forlorn about him; though polite and respectable, he is almost infinitely remote.)*

BARTLEBY. I came in answer…

THE LAWYER. Answer? Oh, yes, the advertisement. Come in, sir. You are a clerk then, a scrivener?

BARTLEBY. I have been that, sir.

THE LAWYER. Well, we are rich here in nothing if not papers for copying.

(sings)

IT'S A SNUG LITTLE PRACTICE,
NOTHING GRAND, BUT A MODEL IN ITS WAY
OF A SNUG LITTLE PRACTICE,
MOST ATTENTIVE TO CLIENTS WHO CAN PAY.
WE ARE KNOWN FOR BEING SAFE, CORRECT, AND DIGNIFIED.
OUR ART IS MAKING SURE THAT WEALTHY CLIENTS ARE CONTENT.

IF WE CARRY OFF OUR PART WITH AN UNDERTAKER'S AIR,
WE HAVE JUSTIFIED THE BILLING OF AN EXTRA TEN PERCENT.

THERE ARE MEN OF THE LAW, VERY CELEBRATED GENTLEMEN YOU READ OF,
SPEAKING GRAVELY IN COURT, WHERE THEIR ARGUMENTS ARE DULY TAKEN HEED OF.
WE ARE NOT OF THEIR KIND, BUT I'M CERTAIN YOU WOULD FIND UPON INQUIRING
THEY HAVE TROUBLES ALL TOO MANY, AND THEY DO NOT MAKE A PENNY MORE THAN SOMEONE MORE RETIRING

WITH A SNUG LITTLE PRACTICE,
NEVER TOUCHED BY THE ISSUES OF THE DAY.
JUST A SNUG LITTLE PRACTICE,
NEVER LACKING FOR CLIENTS WHO CAN PAY
FOR THE HANDLING OF THEIR DEEDS, THEIR BONDS, THEIR MORTGAGES,
THEIR PAPERS TO BE COPIED OUT AND COPIED ONCE AGAIN.
SO WE GET OUR DAILY BREAD IN A TRANQUIL LITTLE WORLD
WHERE THE SOUND OF MAKING MONEY IS THE SCRATCHING OF A PEN,

WHERE FROM EVERY HUMBLE INKWELL OUR ETERNAL LIFEBLOOD POURS.
THERE, I'VE DONE WITH MAKING SPEECHES. HERE'S THE DESK THAT SHALL BE YOURS.
IF EVERYTHING'S AGREEABLE YOU MAY AS WELL COMMENCE.
FOR EVERY HUNDRED WORDS I PAY THE USUAL FOUR CENTS.

(Conversation over, the lawyer would leave. But for a nagging afterthought:)

I do beg your pardon. Your name again, sir?

BARTLEBY. Bartleby.

THE LAWYER. And so Bartleby came into my employ. If he said one word more than that on our first meeting, I cannot now, to save my life, recall it.

(A heavy weight is on him. After a moment he continues.)

Well, it can hardly matter now.

(exit)

Scene Two

*(The other two occupants of the room, **TURKEY** and **NIPPERS**, step forward and address **BARTLEBY**, who throughout all that follows is unresponsive, perhaps overwhelmed.)*

TURKEY.
THERE ARE HARD-WORKING MEN, QUITE INVISIBLE
TO OTHERS, WHO EMPLOY THEM.

NIPPERS.
EVERY DAY WITH A PEN, THEY MAKE PROFITS FOR
THE MEN WHO WILL ENJOY THEM.

TURKEY.
THOUGH BY NOW YOU HAVE SEEN THAT THE WORK
IS PLAINLY MEANINGLESS AND MENIAL,

NIPPERS.
YOUR GOOD SPIRITS OUGHT TO RALLY, KNOWING
PRISONERS AND GALLEY SLAVES HAVE CALLINGS
LESS CONGENIAL

TURKEY & NIPPERS.
THAN A SNUG LITTLE PRACTICE,

NIPPERS.
WHERE YOU'RE WISE IF YOU ALWAYS KNOW YOUR
PLACE,

TURKEY & NIPPERS.
IN A SNUG LITTLE PRACTICE,

TURKEY.
WITH YOUR HUMBLE GOOD HUMOR ON YOUR FACE.

NIPPERS.
IF IT COST YOU HALF YOUR LIFE, YOUR HEALTH,
YOUR DIGNITY,
IF SOMETIMES YOU MAY GRIEVE TO SEE THE LACKEY
YOU'VE BECOME,

TURKEY.
JUST REMEMBER YOUR REWARD AFTER MANY
FRUGAL YEARS:
YOU WILL FIND YOU CAN RETIRE ON A TIDY LITTLE
SUM.

TURKEY & NIPPERS.
> THAT WILL KEEP YOU FROM THE POORHOUSE AS
> YOUR FINAL DAYS GO BY,
> ASSUMING YOU DON'T TAKE BEYOND A YEAR OR SO
> TO DIE.

TURKEY. May I introduce Nippers?

NIPPERS. And you may refer to this gentleman as Turkey.

TURKEY. Nippers is a scrivener at present, but will be mayor one day. Just ask him.

NIPPERS. And Turkey is waiting to come into his fortune and set up as a country squire.

TURKEY. You think, perhaps, the names are out of the ordinary. They are nicknames, of course, of our own devising.

NIPPERS. *(of the* **LAWYER***) He's* used them so long he's forgotten any others we once had.

*(***GINGER NUT*** enters.)*

TURKEY. The boy is called Ginger Nut, and you will find him of great use in procuring the same in the streets nearby. Ginger nut cakes, that is, for your nourishment. Sustain the faculties when dinner time is not yet at hand. But do not be fooled. Ginger Nut will surpass us all shortly. The lad, not the cakes. He is to be a lawyer.

GINGER NUT. My father says *I'm* not growing up to drive a cart.

TURKEY. He'll be a judge upon the bench one day, and cast us all into jail.

NIPPERS. We'll find one for you. A nickname. What do they call you?

BARTLEBY. Bartleby.

*(***TURKEY***,* **NIPPERS***, and* **GINGER NUT** *consider* **BARTLEBY** *critically.)*

TURKEY. Broadsword.

NIPPERS. Herringbone.

GINGER NUT. Half Hitch.

TURKEY. Limestone.

NIPPERS. Hedgehog.

GINGER NUT. Agamemnon.

TURKEY. Yes, I think we shall call you Bartleby.

*(going to the window next to **BARTLEBY**'s desk)*

And you will derive great pleasure from the view out your window: a blank wall not three feet away. Fine old brick, soot, darkness, confinement – all the beauties of a great city. Eh? You're speechless, I see.

*(But **BARTLEBY** seems genuinely interested, not taking the joke.)*

NIPPERS. At least the neighbors will not be complaining of his noise.

TURKEY.
IN THE WORLD OF ODD TRADITIONS THAT THE LAW HAS ALWAYS BEEN,
THE ODDEST THINGS OF ALL

TURKEY, NIPPERS, & GINGER NUT.
ARE THOSE WHO CHOOSE TO WORK HEREIN.

Scene Three

(**THE LAWYER** *is at his desk, in the full enjoyment of life.*)

THE LAWYER. Business at this time was quite brisk, hence the hiring of Bartleby. For I was determined that however much the practice grew, nothing should prevent the door being shut and locked at 6:00 p.m., that I might go to my evening repose or pleasure, and my clerks presumably to theirs, whatever that might be.

NIPPERS. He never asked, and when we told him he forgot.

THE LAWYER. Bartleby joined our family here, one might say, and all was well at first. He did an extraordinary quantity of writing, as if long famishing for something to do. He never left his desk, but cheerfully subsisted – in the case of Bartleby we may as well strike the word "cheerful" – on those small cakes called ginger nuts, brought to him daily by our industrious office boy. An excellent boy there, most promising.

GINGER NUT. He was like a writing engine. Shovel a little fuel in and you'd get papers out of him all day. Light a candle and he'd go all night too.

THE LAWYER. I began to rely on his accuracy, to approve of his silence, and to wish I had a whole office of Bartlebys.

NIPPERS. Then one day the earth stopped turning.

TURKEY. Time stood still.

GINGER NUT. The sun went dark.

THE LAWYER. Bartleby, Monday's testimony has been copied. Come help me correct it.

BARTLEBY. I would prefer not to.

(silence)

THE LAWYER. Momentarily stunned, I then realized of course that Bartleby had entirely mistaken my meaning, or I his response. I repeated the request.

BARTLEBY. I would prefer not to.

THE LAWYER. Is the man mad?

*(**NIPPERS** nudges **TURKEY** to watch and see what will happen. **GINGER NUT** catches the gesture and begins to watch as well, with high hopes of being entertained.)*

Examining documents is a necessary duty. One person takes the original, others take the copies, one reads aloud. From the beginning of time it has been so. I sometimes do it myself.

BARTLEBY. I would prefer not to.

TURKEY. He'll never stand for this. The man is doomed.

NIPPERS. Blood will flow today.

THE LAWYER. Such was Bartleby's reply on that day and every other. He would not examine documents. And that was not all he refused. I might say, "Bartleby, will you step round to the post office?"

BARTLEBY. I would prefer not to.

THE LAWYER. It is but a three minutes' walk!

*(No further reply from **BARTLEBY**)*

To this and other requests of the most ordinary sort came this extraordinary reply. Now, if there had been any touch of insolence about the man I should have violently dismissed him from the premises.

*(**TURKEY**, **NIPPERS**, and **GINGER NUT** think the show may now begin.)*

But no, one could almost see him considering any request made of him, even admitting its merits, only to remain at last unmoved.

BARTLEBY. At present I would prefer not to.

*(**BARTLEBY** turns to stare out his window, and **THE LAWYER** in frustration lets the matter drop.)*

GINGER NUT. He *will* stand for it!

THE LAWYER. I cursed myself often, in vain. And more than once in the press of business, it was *I* who went to the post office and Bartleby who remained at his desk!

(exit)

TURKEY. *(rising from his desk)* It's twelve o'clock, Nippers. Shall we ask Bartleby to dine with us?

NIPPERS. One might as well ask the wall to dine. Bartleby is a man of two talents only: He copies documents or he stares out the window.

GINGER NUT. At a wall!

NIPPERS. Ginger Nut, what is the probable effect of staring at a brick wall for ten hours in the week?

GINGER NUT. You'd start giving names to the flies.

NIPPERS. The correct answer is: loss of employment.
> THIS CAN'T GO ON.
> HE'LL SOON BE GONE.
> ONE DOES NOT PAY A MAN HIS WAGE
> TO STARE AT WALLS.
> OR TO DISDAINFULLY REFUSE
> WHEN DUTY CALLS.

TURKEY.
> A MAN MAY BE A BIT ECCENTRIC,
> AND THERE'S LITTLE HARM IN THAT.

NIPPERS.
> A SHIRKER'S NO MORE WELCOME IN AN OFFICE
> THAN A RAT.
> HE'LL SOON BE GONE.
> THIS CAN'T GO ON.

TURKEY.
> HE ISN'T WELL.
> WE ALL CAN TELL.
> HE'S SLIGHTLY MAD AND CANNOT
> CALL HIS MIND HIS OWN.

NIPPERS.
> HE'S ONLY MAD WHEN HE PREFERS
> TO BE ALONE.

GINGER NUT.
> HAS HE ESCAPED FROM SOME ASYLUM?
> WILL THEY COME AND TAKE HIM BACK?

NIPPERS.
> IF ANYONE WILL HAVE HIM,

> I'LL BE FIRST TO HELP HIM PACK.
> LET HIM GO WELL,
> AND ROT IN HELL.

TURKEY. Nippers, the child.

GINGER NUT. Nippers, the child.

NIPPERS.
> IT'S GALLING HOW HE LIVES A LIFE OF LEISURE.
> DO *I* HAVE ALL THESE PRIVILEGES? DO *YOU*?
> DOES SOMEONE ASK ME, "SIR, WHAT IS YOUR PLEASURE?
> WHAT DO YOU CHOOSE TO DO,
> OR REFUSE TO DO?"

TURKEY.
> WHY IS IT SO?
> WE CANNOT KNOW.
> BUT OUR EMPLOYER HAS RESOLVED
> TO LET HIM STAY.

GINGER NUT.
> I COULD HAVE SWORN HE'D THROW HIM
> OUT OF DOORS TODAY.

TURKEY.
> IT MAY BE BARTLEBY'S THE NEPHEW
> OF AN OLD AND WORTHY FRIEND.
> OR SOME OBSCURE RELATION OF HIS OWN
> HE MUST DEFEND.
> IT COULD BE SO.
> WE CANNOT KNOW.

> *(They all stare at each other a moment and consider the possibilities.)*

GINGER NUT. Bastard son more likely.

TURKEY. *(Hastily steering **GINGER NUT** to the door as all three leave for midday dinner. To **NIPPERS**:)* You've been a terrible influence on the boy.

NIPPERS. I'm very sorry. I'll pay for his beer today.

> *(All but **BARTLEBY** leave.)*

Scene Four

(**BARTLEBY** *stands suddenly, staring out the window that commands a view of nothing but the wall of the adjoining building. During the following, the* **LAWYER** *will reenter the office, without being noticed, and stand motionless, watching him.*)

BARTLEBY.

A WALL OF BRICK,
GROWN BLACK WITH TIME,
ALL DARK AND COLD,
UNCHANGING.

A WALL OF BRICK
THAT ONCE WAS EARTH,
THAT ONCE WAS CLAY,
THAT ONCE WAS SOFT AND CHANGEABLE,
AND MIGHT YET HAVE BEEN TURNED
TO ANYTHING.

DRAWN FROM THE EARTH,
AND PRESSED INTO MOLDS,
PRESSED INTO PERFECT SAMENESS,
DRIED AND STACKED
AND FINALLY TRANSFORMED
BY FIRE.

IT WILL CHANGE NO MORE.
IT IS CLAY NO MORE.
FOREVER FIXED,
UNIFORM AND HARD.
IT NOW IS BRICK,
ALL DARK AND COLD,
THE FIRE LONG GONE.

THE YEARS WILL PASS,
IT WILL NOT FALL,
IT WILL NOT CHANGE,
THIS DEAD, UNYIELDING WALL.

Scene Five

(**BARTLEBY** *is now silent but still frozen at the window.*
THE LAWYER *still watches him, fascinated.*)

(*Suddenly* **BARTLEBY** *sits, and the action is so unexpected that* **THE LAWYER** *almost jumps, then comes to his senses and hurries to busy himself with his papers.*)

THE LAWYER. Granted that Bartleby sometimes fell into odd reveries at his window, he was otherwise useful to me, not argumentative, honest, industrious, and *always there*, first in the morning, last at night. But sometimes, much to my discredit, I found myself laying traps for him, as if provoking him to defy me.

BARTLEBY, THESE PAPERS,
COME HELP ME TO INSPECT THEM.

BARTLEBY.

I WOULD PREFER NOT TO.

THE LAWYER. (*aside*)

IT'S PLAIN HE WILL REFUSE
ANY TASK OF ANY SORT.

(*to* **BARTLEBY**)

WON'T YOU FIND THE COPIES?
I'M READY TO CORRECT THEM.

BARTLEBY.

I WOULD PREFER NOT TO.

THE LAWYER. (*aside*)

HOW *DID* I FALL SO LOW
AS TO TAKE THIS FOR MY SPORT?

(*to* **BARTLEBY**)

WILL YOU PASS MY NOTES TO TURKEY AT HIS PLACE?
WILL YOU FILE AWAY THIS PAPER WITH THE REST?
WILL YOU GIVE ME ANY HINT OF WHO YOU ARE?

BARTLEBY.

I WOULD PREFER –

THE LAWYER. (*dangerously*)

VERY GOOD, SIR.
VERY GOOD INDEED, SIR.

And if ever I had thought of an action to match the self-assurance of my tone, Bartleby would have regretted it very much.

(**TURKEY** and **NIPPERS** *return to their usual places and* **THE LAWYER** *is very aware of them.*)

My other clerks watched to see what I would do, and for some weeks I did nothing, half pleased with my liberality and half ashamed. But some things could not be ignored, and who was to be master after all?

TURKEY. Sir, would you prefer to have this on your desk before I leave today?

THE LAWYER. So you have got it too!

TURKEY. Got what?

THE LAWYER. The word. That word.

NIPPERS. The second copy can go on blue, if you prefer.

THE LAWYER. That's the one!

TURKEY. Prefer? Oh yes, queer word. I never use it myself.

GINGER NUT. (*entering*) I can go to the post office now, sir, if you prefer.

THE LAWYER. Thank you, I do not!

(*to* **BARTLEBY**, *who faces away and does not react at all.*)

You hear? You have turned the very tongues of my clerks. What next? Will everyone become demented and start laying down extraordinary conditions for his employment?

(*to* **TURKEY** *and* **NIPPERS** *with a touch of pleading*)

IN A SNUG LITTLE PRACTICE,
DOES A CLERK NOT PERFORM FROM DAY TO DAY
FOR THE SAKE OF THE PRACTICE
ANY TRIFLING REQUEST THAT COMES HIS WAY?

Mr. Nippers?

NIPPERS. You should throw him out of doors, sir.

THE LAWYER. Turkey?

TURKEY. Certainly that's what anyone else would do.

THE LAWYER. And would have done long since!

TURKEY. Yes, sir.

THE LAWYER. Well, then. Really, it's all for the best.

> (*to* **TURKEY**, **NIPPERS**, *and* **GINGER NUT**, *as if somehow needing their approval*)
>
> THIS MAN WAS NEVER MEANT TO BE A SCRIVENER.
> IT UNBALANCES HIS THOUGHT, AS WE HAVE FOUND.
> THIS NEEDN'T BE UNPLEASANT, I CAN PROMISE YOU.
> WE'LL BE PERFECTLY FRATERNAL ALL AROUND.
>
> (**THE LAWYER** *goes to* **BARTLEBY** *and shakes his hand.* **BARTLEBY** *throughout the following does not move or react.*)
>
> WELL DONE.

THE LAWYER, TURKEY, NIPPERS, & GINGER NUT.
> WELL DONE.

THE LAWYER.
> YOU HAVE MADE A GREAT SUCCESS.
> LOOK BACK FONDLY ON YOUR WORK HERE,
> I IMPLORE YOU.

THE LAWYER, TURKEY, NIPPERS, & GINGER NUT.
> WE IMPLORE YOU.

THE LAWYER.
> GOOD LUCK.

THE LAWYER, TURKEY, NIPPERS, & GINGER NUT.
> GODSPEED,

THE LAWYER.
> AS YOU SEEK A NEW ADDRESS

THE LAWYER, TURKEY, NIPPERS, & GINGER NUT.
> FOR THE MANY FINE ENDEAVORS
> YET BEFORE YOU.

GINGER NUT.
> YET BEFORE YOU.

THE LAWYER.
> I OWE YOU THESE TWELVE DOLLARS.
> LET ME GIVE YOU THIRTY-TWO.
> AND WITH THAT MY HEARTY THANKS
> FOR ALL YOU'VE DONE HERE.

THE LAWYER, TURKEY, NIPPERS, & GINGER NUT.

ALL YOU'VE DONE HERE.
THE LAWYER.
YOU NEEDN'T FEEL INDEBTED.
IT'S NO MORE THAN I SHOULD DO.
TURKEY, NIPPERS, & GINGER NUT.
DO NOT LOOK FOR CONTRADICTION;
THERE IS NONE HERE.
THE LAWYER. *(with emphasis)*
THOUGH YOU PART FROM US
AT SIX O'CLOCK THIS DAY,
TURKEY, NIPPERS, & GINGER NUT.
THIS VERY DAY.
THE LAWYER.
WE CAN PROMISE THAT YOUR MEMORY WILL
THE LAWYER, TURKEY, NIPPERS, & GINGER NUT.
NEVER FADE AWAY.
TURKEY, NIPPERS, & GINGER NUT.
SO FARE YOU WELL, GOOD SIR.
THE LAWYER.
WE WILL SEE YOU THEN NO MORE.
TURKEY, NIPPERS, & GINGER NUT.
FARE YOU WELL, GOOD SIR.
THE LAWYER.
SLIDE YOUR KEY BENEATH THE DOOR.
NIPPERS & GINGER NUT.
FARE YOU WELL,
THE LAWYER, TURKEY, NIPPERS, & GINGER NUT.
SAY WE ALL,
FARE YOU WELL.
FARE YOU WELL, SAY WE ALL,
FARE YOU WELL.
FARE YOU WELL.

THE LAWYER. *(putting on his hat and leaving as quickly as possible without betraying the fact that he is fleeing the scene)*
And so with his dismissal, on the best of terms, I brought the distressing matter of Bartleby skillfully to a close.

NIPPERS. *(Sardonic? Me?)* The next day.

(THE LAWYER enters and sees BARTLEBY.)

THE LAWYER. Good god. Not gone?

Scene Six

(The same. Yes, exactly the same. **TURKEY**, **NIPPERS**, *and* **GINGER NUT** *at their places,* **BARTLEBY** *staring at the wall.)*

THE LAWYER. *(almost despairing)*
SUCH A SNUG LITTLE PRACTICE,
NOTHING GRAND, BUT A MODEL IN ITS WAY
OF A SNUG LITTLE PRACTICE...

Plainly Bartleby, not I, was to make the decisions in my office. There was but one thing to do.

(to **BARTLEBY***)*

Well, Bartleby, perhaps it is a providence after all. I have some hundred pages of testimony to be copied in the next three or four days' time. If I have been over hasty with you I frankly ask your pardon. Let you take your accustomed place then and continue your work.

BARTLEBY. I have decided upon doing no more writing.

THE LAWYER. No more? Do no more writing? And pray, what is the reason?

BARTLEBY. Do you not see the reason?

(He looks at the **LAWYER**.*)*

THE LAWYER. His eyes were inflamed, no doubt from an excess of copy work over these first weeks in poor light. He has blinded himself in service to me! What answer can I make to that?

(to **BARTLEBY**, *who has returned to his wall)*

Bartleby, you shall desist from writing at present, and use the occasion to take wholesome exercise in the open air.

BARTLEBY.
A WALL OF BRICK,
GROWN BLACK WITH TIME,

THE LAWYER. *(retreating to his own desk, his mind melting)*
God, I am a fool and I confess it!

Scene Seven

NIPPERS. Within a few days his eyes were perfectly normal.

TURKEY. But still he did not write.

THE LAWYER. It was clear to all how little I ruled my own life. I was reduced to being counseled by Ginger Nut, the office boy.

GINGER NUT. He never *does* anything, sir. I think he's a little loony. You should turn him out, sir.

THE LAWYER. I certainly believed I had done so.

GINGER NUT. I can go for the police. They'll settle with him.

THE LAWYER. Settle?

GINGER NUT. They'll take him up before the judge for vagrancy.

THE LAWYER. Ah, you have learned a new word.

GINGER NUT. Hundreds of 'em.

THE LAWYER. And the knowledge of when to use them?

GINGER NUT. (*singsong, delightedly ticking them off on his fingers*) Vagrancy, trespass, infringement, encroachment...

THE LAWYER. That will do.

GINGER NUT. Idling, loitering, unlawful detainer...

THE LAWYER. That will do!

(**GINGER NUT** *leaves.*)

Annoying boy. Bartleby, won't you come here a moment? Bartleby.

(**BARTLEBY** *approaches.*)

Suppose your eyesight recovered. Suppose it became better than it ever was before. Would you still do no copying?

BARTLEBY. I have given up copying.

THE LAWYER. Bartleby...you have not been ill treated. Could you not begin now to be a little reasonable?

BARTLEBY. At present I would prefer not to be a little reasonable.

THE LAWYER. This cannot be endured! Then you must quit me at once.

BARTLEBY. I would prefer not to quit you.

THE LAWYER. You should know I have been advised that the police could be sent for. Understand, I would not take such an action lightly. I would prefer not to.

(He gives way almost to a scream on hearing his own words, and proceeds to a tantrum.)

Aaaaaagh!

TELL ME, BY WHAT EARTHLY RIGHT
DO YOU PROPOSE TO STAY?
YOU DO NO WORK, YOU PAY NO RENT,
YOU DAYDREAM TO YOUR HEART'S CONTENT,
AND THUS YOUR TIME AND MINE IS SPENT
FROM DAY TO BLESSED DAY.

SO BEGONE, MAN.
JUST BEGONE.
THE WEEK IS DONE, AND I'M AFRAID
SO IS YOUR TIME HERE.
I TRULY SWEAR YOU WON'T BE PAID
ANOTHER DIME HERE.
WELL, NOT WHILE I'M HERE.
YOU MUST BEGONE!

NO ONE'S EVER MADE ME
SO UPSET AND OVERWROUGHT.
YOU DO JUST WHAT YOU CHOOSE TO DO.
WHAT THEN OF ALL THE OTHERS WHO
WILL THINK THAT THEY CAN DO SO TOO?
I SHUDDER AT THE THOUGHT.

SO BEGONE, MAN.
JUST BEGONE.
I GIVE YOU WARNING I WILL HEAR
OF NO POSTPONEMENT,
NO FALLING ILL, NO LOOKING QUEER,
AND NO ATONEMENT.
THIS IS DISOWNMENT.
YOU MUST BEGONE!

(He leaves in a passion.)

Scene Eight

(Sudden peace, for it is Sunday, and the church calls.)

THE LAWYER. The next morning, which was a Sunday, I happened to go to Trinity Church, to hear a celebrated preacher, and finding myself rather early on the ground, I thought I would walk round to my chambers. Upon trying my key in the door…

(He does.)

It was stopped up from within.

BARTLEBY. *(peeking out the door)* I am sorry, sir.

THE LAWYER. Bartleby!

BARTLEBY. I think if you will walk around the block two or three times, I will have concluded my business.

THE LAWYER. I was unmanned; I slunk away from my own door.

(He walks, disputing with himself.)

Bartleby, in my office of a Sunday morning, in his shirt sleeves! Doing what? It was not to be thought for a moment that Bartleby was an immoral person. Working then? No, he would be the last man to sit down to his desk in any state approaching to nudity. And let me not forget, as *he* must have done, he was my employee no longer!

(back at the door)

Five minutes later, my key turned in the lock and I entered. In these many weeks I had not once seen my office without Bartleby in his usual corner. But this time I was quite alone.

(It is his own office, but he is awestruck by what he sees, and he moves slowly, like a man uncovering a sacred archeological site.)

A FAINT IMPRESSION ON THE SOFA. IT IS HIS BED.
A BLANKET TIGHTLY ROLLED BENEATH HIS DESK.
A BASIN AND A RAGGED TOWEL, A BIT OF SOAP.
GOOD GOD, HE MAKES HIS HOME HERE.

THE LAWYER *(cont.)*
> AND THIS WAS HERE.
> THIS ALL WAS HERE TO SEE.

*(He opens **BARTLEBY**'s desk.)*

> WITHIN HIS DESK, NO CLUE TO WHO HE IS.
> AMONG THE TIDY PAPERS, BUT TWO THINGS THAT
> ARE HIS:

(A folded sheet of newspaper)

> HIS DINNER, THESE FEW CRUMBS OF CHEESE AND
> GINGER NUTS,

(A knotted bandanna)

> AND ALL HE HAS OF MONEY IN THE WORLD.

> AND THIS WAS HERE.
> THIS ALL WAS HERE TO SEE.
> AND DID I SEE?

(Trying anger, trying pity. Nothing quite fits.)

> THIS MAN, THIS BURDEN GROWN UNBEARABLE,
> THIS WRETCHED CREATURE UTTERLY ALONE.
> THIS MAN, WHO LIVES UPON MY KINDNESS,
> IF KINDNESS BE THE WORD – OR RATHER
> FOOLISHNESS.
> FOR HE PREYS UPON ME, THERE'S THE TRUTH.
> HE PLAYS ME FOR A FOOL!
> WHO ELSE WOULD SO INDULGE THE MAN?

> That's it – if I did not, who else would save him?

*(looking out on **BARTLEBY**'s wall)*

> IN THE EVENING, WHEN THE STREET IS FULL
> OF PEOPLE GOING HOME,
> DOES HE STAND HERE?
> DOES HE LISTEN TO THE CRIES
> OF THOSE WHO KNOW WHERE THEY ARE BOUND?
> IS HE COMFORTED PERHAPS,
> OR IS HE WOUNDED BY THE SOUND?
> DOES HE STAND AND STARE AT NOTHING BUT A
> WALL?

THE LAWYER *(cont.)*
> BUT SURELY HE WAS ONCE A VERY DIFFERENT MAN,
> WHO KNEW OF LIFE BEYOND THIS BARREN ROOM.
>
> *(sitting at **BARTLEBY**'s place)*
>
> WHEN IT'S NIGHTTIME, AND THE STREET IS BARE,
> AND DAWN IS HOURS AWAY,
> DOES HE SIT HERE?
> DOES HE TUMBLE INTO MADNESS,
> OR JUST BALANCE ON THE BRINK?
> DOES HE THINK UPON HIS CARES,
> OR IS IT BETTER NOT TO THINK?
> DOES HE SIT AND WAIT FOR TIME ITSELF TO END?
>
> *(rising, taking in the office again)*
>
> YES, SURELY I WAS ONCE A VERY DIFFERENT MAN,
> WHO KNEW OF LIFE BEYOND THIS BARREN ROOM.
>
> VERY WELL, THEN, SIR, VERY WELL.
> FOR HOWEVER LONG YOU PLEASE, YOU ARE TO STAY.
> AND IF MY CLIENTS AND MY COLLEAGUES TAKE TO LAUGHING UP THEIR SLEEVE,
> AS THEY MAY, THEN THEY MAY.
>
> FOR CHARITY I BORE WITH YOU FOR EIGHT HOURS IN THE DAY,
> REPAID BY TREATMENT I COULD NOT ABIDE.
> IT OUGHT TO BE FAR WORSE TO FIND YOU MINE ALL FOUR-AND-TWENTY,
> AND YET, THE DEBT HAS PASSED TO THE OTHER SIDE.

Scene Nine

(The office on a Monday morning. All but **GINGER NUT** *are present.)*

TURKEY. But Sunday cannot last forever, nor Sunday resolutions. At least in my experience, the next thing after Sunday…is Monday.

NIPPERS. The neighborhood was talking, and we made sure our employer knew of it. The other gentlemen in the buildings nearby, their clerks, even their scrubwomen, told one another that we kept a strange fellow here who refused all work and was probably deranged.

TURKEY. Not good for business. A possible client may think twice.

NIPPERS. May look elsewhere.

TURKEY. May tell others.

GINGER NUT. *(entering)* Message from Mr. Bramble, sir. Please keep your appointment today at *his* office.

THE LAWYER. Not mine?

GINGER NUT. *(with a glance at* **BARTLEBY***)* He says the climate here does his health no good.

THE LAWYER. Cancel the appointment.

GINGER NUT. Yes, sir.

THE LAWYER. No! It's no matter to me. I will walk to his office.

TURKEY. Sir, I feel it a solemn duty to mention a riddle often heard these days in the public house, though *I* do not find it humorous –

THE LAWYER. I need not hear it, thank you.

NIPPERS. A scrivener from Mr. Sunderman's made up a ditty and was actually singing it in the street: "I would prefer not to." Of course I stopped him at once.

TURKEY. What begins in jest will end in earnest, and it will cost you greatly, sir.

THE LAWYER. *(narrating)* It was a difficult time. Business did seem in decline. Perhaps the reason was to be found staring out the window. And perhaps my clients could see that I myself was not at my best. But surely Bartleby would soon return to his former self, and so might we all.

*(to **BARTLEBY**)*

Is there any little thing you will do, Bartleby? Anything at all. Copy a small paper perhaps.

BARTLEBY. I would prefer not to.

THE LAWYER. *(narrating)* At all events, between Turkey, Nippers, and that infuriating office boy –

GINGER NUT. *(memorizing, dictionary in hand)* Derangement, lunacy, mental incapacity, non compos mentis –

THE LAWYER. Compassion!

(GINGER NUT *hesitates, looks at the dictionary as if to turn to C. The* **LAWYER** *snatches the book from his hand.)*

GINGER NUT. Mr. Nippers is waiting for his apple!

(He flees.)

THE LAWYER. At last I could not be deaf to the whispers, and a great change came over me. Bartleby was not old. Suppose he were to live another forty years. Yes, and keep occupying my chambers and scandalizing my professional reputation, and in the end outlive me, and claim possession of my office by right of perpetual occupancy! No, twice before I had tried and failed, but this time the deed must be done. I would naturally give Bartleby money, or write him a fine character reference, or do anything else within my power. But first …Bartleby!

(BARTLEBY *comes silently into view and remains attentive but passive.)*

Bartleby, my good name has become such that…You will admit that certain usages of society must be followed…Please understand, I cannot be ruined for you! I can't be ruined for you, sir!

(He hadn't meant to raise his voice, but...well, there it is.)

I mean that I am resolved and you must comply. You must, in short...you *must*...

(A new thought occurs.)

...understand...that I am moving my office to new premises. It is too crowded here. The air is bad. Tomorrow morning I will have men here with carts. And I will not require your services in my new place of business. I encourage you to...I beg you to seek another place.

*(**BARTLEBY** and the **LAWYER** are frozen in place.)*

Scene Ten

(There is a rush of activity by **TURKEY**, **NIPPERS**, *and* **GINGER NUT**, *with the sudden happiness of a great weight being lifted, as they move all the furnishings out.)*

*(***BARTLEBY** *remains motionless at his window, untouched by the activity around him. Oddly, the* **LAWYER** *is in much the same condition, barely watching the proceedings.)*

(At last, the room being empty, **TURKEY** *goes to the* **LAWYER** *and touches him on the shoulder, jolting him back to consciousness. The* **LAWYER** *goes to* **BARTLEBY** *but cannot speak, and instead puts money in his hand then tears himself from the scene.)*

(A change of light, **BARTLEBY** *disappears, and the moving scene is replayed in reverse, at double speed. All the same furnishings are brought into the new chambers, and placed in new locations.)*

(At the conclusion of this activity, all are seated at their desks.)

Scene Eleven

(The new office. The clock ticks.)

THE LAWYER. *(A bundle of nerves, tapping his fingers, biting his nails, watching the door.)*
IT'S A SNUG LITTLE PRACTICE,
NOTHING GRAND, BUT –

(He stops to listen. Nothing is there.)

BUT A MODEL IN ITS WAY

NIPPERS. A change of scene is said to be good for a man's nerves.

*(***GINGER NUT***, entering behind the* **LAWYER**, *knocks on his desk or a partition beside it.)*

THE LAWYER. Ahhh!

NIPPERS. It was not so with our employer.

GINGER NUT. Any letters going out, sir?

THE LAWYER. No. Or rather yes. Thank you.

(He hands over the letters.)

TURKEY. He was quite different from his previous self.

NIPPERS. As if expecting at any moment a caller.

GINGER NUT. Or a ghost.

NIPPERS. But for a week or so, all was well.

TURKEY. Then one day a visitor came, a portly man of middle age.

THE LAWYER. My heart stopped when I saw it was the landlord of my old building.

TURKEY. *(facing front, but speaking the part of the landlord.)* That *man*, sir –

THE LAWYER. *(starting)* Man?

TURKEY. Did you not leave behind a man?

THE LAWYER. A man?

TURKEY. When you moved. A man who does not leave, who will not work. He says he prefers not to.

THE LAWYER. Ah. That may be Bartleby.

TURKEY. Who the devil is he?

THE LAWYER. Truly sir, I don't know.

TURKEY. Your apprentice?

THE LAWYER. No.

TURKEY. Clerk?

THE LAWYER. Formerly. *Formerly.*

TURKEY. The other tenants will stand it no longer. He sits on the banisters by day and sleeps in the entry by night. Everyone is in fear of him. There may soon be a mob. And you, sir, you left him.

THE LAWYER. No, I didn't.

TURKEY. You didn't leave him?

THE LAWYER. Well, yes. Yes, I –

TURKEY. Then you must take him away.

THE LAWYER. No, he is nothing to me. Nothing. No more than to you, sir, or your tenants. I employed him, I dismissed him, I…I left him.

TURKEY. Hmph. Then since evidently you will not, *I* will have him dealt with.

THE LAWYER. No. Let me speak to him, sir. I will come to you this afternoon.

Scene Twelve

(A stairway landing at the old building, where **BARTLEBY** *sits on a banister.)*

THE LAWYER. At the old building, he sat upon the banister outside my former chambers.

(to **BARTLEBY***)*

Bartleby, do you know you are the cause of great tribulation to me, remaining here after being dismissed from the office?

(silence)

One of two things must take place. Either you must do something, or something must be done to you.

(silence)

Surely there are many other places you would prefer to go.

BARTLEBY. No, I would prefer not to make any change.

THE LAWYER.
THE WORLD'S VERY LARGE, AS YOU HARDLY CAN KNOW.
I KNEW LITTLE WHEN I WAS THAT YOUNG.
NEW ROADS LIE BEFORE YOU, WHEREVER YOU GO.
YOU MAY FOLLOW THEM ALL WHEN YOU'RE YOUNG.
A YOUNG MAN HAS DREAMS THAT MAY YET COME TO BE.
THERE'S VIEWING GREAT CITIES OR GOING TO SEA.
THOUGH THE WORLD GIVES YOU ONLY A FUTURE TO CHASE,
IT'S A VERY FINE PLACE TO BE YOUNG.

Perhaps a clerkship in a dry-goods store. Or a bartender's business. There is no trying of the eyesight in that. Or you might travel through the country collecting bills for the merchants. That would improve your health. Or go as a companion to Europe, to entertain some young gentleman with your conversation. How would that suit you?

BARTLEBY. *(scarcely audible)* I would prefer –

THE LAWYER.

> A YOUNG MAN HAS DREAMS THAT MAY YET COME TO BE.
> THERE'S VIEWING GREAT CITIES OR GOING TO SEA.
> THOUGH THE WORLD GIVES YOU ONLY A FUTURE TO CHASE,
> IT'S A VERY FINE PLACE TO BE YOUNG.
> IT'S A VERY FINE PLACE TO BE YOUNG.

Well, Bartleby?

BARTLEBY. No, I like to be stationary.

*(It takes the **LAWYER** a moment to face his final defeat, but he does.)*

THE LAWYER. Stationary. Stationary you shall be then.

(He starts to leave, but then stops a long while, and finally turns back.)

Bartleby, will you go home with me now, not to my office, but my dwelling, and remain there until we may conclude upon some better arrangement? Come, let us go now, right away.

BARTLEBY. At present I would prefer not to make any change at all.

*(The **LAWYER** has no more words. Fighting what might as well be physical pain, he breaks from the scene.)*

*(The music erupts into chaos, and it is several moments before it resolves to the point where the **LAWYER** can speak, then it continues throughout the following, becoming ever calmer.)*

THE LAWYER. I suppose for twenty years past I had not broken into a full run, but I ran that day like a madman, up Wall Street towards Broadway, jumping into the first omnibus, certain of being pursued by – I knew not what. In an instant I resolved to leave the city. I think I was scarcely rational, for I spent several days in my carriage merely driving without aim through the far suburbs and nearby towns. This I did until at last I felt I was quite myself again.

Scene Thirteen

(Limbo)

THE LAWYER. On my return to the city, I was told that Bartleby had been taken to prison as a vagrant. I felt wretched at the news. And then, strangely, I did not. Surely this was no great change for a man like Bartleby. Had he not been in prison all along?

I called at the Tombs – or to speak more properly, the Halls of Justice – and was admitted to see him. I am pleased to recall that I paid out some few pieces of silver to have his food increased, and improved, although from everything I was told, he never ate. But in truth, I did pay...

And I went often to see him. Well, twice it may have been. If only he had spoken to me, I would have seen much more of him, business permitting. I would have written to any friends he could have named, or put in a word somewhere, anywhere at all...What would I not have done?

As things were, though, my business was pressing, Bartleby would not speak...and perhaps a deal of time went by without my notice.

But one day I did find myself near the Tombs on another matter, and asking after my former scrivener, I was advised to seek him in the prison yard, where he would undoubtedly be found staring at the wall.

And so he was. He lay on his side in a small patch of prison grass and indeed he stared at the wall. But he was dead.

Scene Fourteen

(The office. All are present except **GINGER NUT.***)*

BARTLEBY.
> IN TIME THERE CAME TO LIGHT A CERTAIN STORY,
> MAYBE TRUE AND MAYBE NOT. IT TOLD OF
> BARTLEBY.
> HIS JOB FOR SOME YEARS PAST WAS THAT OF POSTAL
> CLERK,
> A SORT OF SUB-ASSISTANT FOR DEAD LETTERS.
>
> THERE HE WATCHED DAY BY DAY
> AT HIS DEAD LETTER DESK
> ALL THAT PASSED THROUGH HIS HANDS
> TO THE FLAMES.
>
> *(with growing passion)*
>
> WORDS OF LOVE,

THE LAWYER.
> WORDS OF LOVE,

BARTLEBY.
> WORDS OF LONGING,

THE LAWYER.
> HOPE AND LONGING,

BARTLEBY.
> OF FORGIVENESS COME TOO LATE,

THE LAWYER.
> MEANT FOR EYES THAT NOW WERE SHUT,

BOTH.
> EAGER WORDS THAT COULD NOT REACH
> A HUMAN HEART.

BARTLEBY.
> ALL THIS HE BURNED,
> DAY AFTER DAY.
> IT WAS HIS JOB.
>
> *(He is overcome.)*

THE LAWYER.
> HOW ODD, HOW VERY ODD,

THAT STIFLED HOPES
COULD PROVE THEMSELVES
SO HEAVY,
THAT WORDS UNHEARD
COULD WEIGH ENOUGH
TO CRUSH A MAN.

BARTLEBY. *(very composed again)*
THAT WAS ALL THE STORY TOLD,
AND WHETHER TRUE OR NOT,
IT COULD MATTER NOW TO BARTLEBY NO MORE.

(He turns away.)

NIPPERS. A snug little practice, that's what he used to call it. Scarcely a fit place to work now. I may soon be forced to consider other offers.

TURKEY. Only last week, he dismissed poor Ginger Nut, pretending to find fault with his work. I went to him and frankly said, "You'll not find a better boy than that, nor one more eager to tread your footsteps." He answered only,

TURKEY & THE LAWYER. "I know."

NIPPERS. Since that time, he's been a little deranged.

TURKEY. And spends all too much time staring at the wall.

*(But the **LAWYER** is not depressed; one might almost say elated.)*

THE LAWYER.
THERE IS A CHAIN
WE CALL HUMANITY.
AND WHEN IT BREAKS, A MAN CAN LOSE
A THING HE NEEDS AS MUCH AS AIR.

AM I THE ONLY ONE NOW WHO CAN SEE?
OR THE ONLY ONE WHO DIDN'T SEE BEFORE?

HOW ODD IT IS.
HOW VERY CURIOUS.

How extraordinary!

The End

OTHER TITLES AVAILABLE FROM SAMUEL FRENCH

DEAD CITY
Sheila Callaghan

Full Length / Comic Drama / 3m, 4f / Unit Set

It's June 16, 2004. Samantha Blossom, a chipper woman in her 40s, wakes up one June morning in her Upper East Side apartment to find her life being narrated over the airwaves of public radio. She discovers in the mail an envelope addressed to her husband from his lover, which spins her raw and untethered into an odyssey through the city...a day full of chance encounters, coincidences, a quick love affair, and a fixation on the mysterious Jewel Jupiter. Jewel, the young but damaged poet genius, eventually takes a shine to Samantha and brings her on a midnight tour of the meat-packing district which changes Samantha's life forever—or doesn't. This 90 minute comic drama is a modernized, gender-reversed, relocated, hyper-theatrical riff on the novel *Ulysses*, occurring exactly 100 years to the day after Joyce's jaunt through Dublin.

"Wonderful...Sheila Callaghan's pleasingly witty and theatrical new drama that is a love letter to New York masquerading as hate mail...[Callaghan] writes with a world-weary tone and has a poet's gift for economical description.
The entire dead city comes alive..."
- *The New York Times*

"*Dead City,* Sheila Callaghan's riff on James Joyce's *Ulysses* is stylish, lyrical, fascinating, occasionally irritating, and eminently worthwhile...the kind of work that is thoroughly invigorating."
- *Back Stage*

SAMUELFRENCH.COM

OTHER TITLES AVAILABLE FROM SAMUEL FRENCH

JACK GOES BOATING
Bob Glaudini

Full Length / Comedy / 2m, 2f / Interior
Four flawed but likeable lower/middle-class New Yorkers interact in a touching and warm-hearted play about learning how to stay afloat in the deep water of day-to-day living. Laced with cooking classes, swimming lessons and a smorgasbord of illegal drugs, *Jack Goes Boating* is a story of date panic, marital meltdown, betrayal, and the prevailing grace of the human spirit.

"An immensely likable play [that] exudes a wry compassion."
- *The New York Times*

"Endearing romantic comedy about a married couple and the social-misfit friends they fix up. Witty and knowing and all heart."
- *Variety*

"Glides effortlessly from the shallow end of the emotional pool to the deep end."
- *Theatremania.com*

SAMUELFRENCH.COM